THE ANDERSONVILLE TRIAL

BY SAUL LEVITT

DRAMATISTS
PLAY SERVICE
INC.

For Dena

The basic source material for this play is the official record of the actual trial of Henry Wirz, which took place in Washington, D.C., in the summer of 1865. It may be considered "documentary" to the following extent: that it is set in the time and place circumstance of the historical trial; that the formal roles and names of its characters repeat those of the historical participants; and that some of the dialogue derives from the trial record. Apart from the foregoing factual aspect it expresses the author's own conception of the personalities and the occasion—and is to be read as a "play" and not a "documentary."

THE ANDERSONVILLE TRIAL
Copyright © Renewed 1988, Dena Levitt and Dan David Levitt
Copyright © 1960, Samuel Levitt

All Rights Reserved

CAST OF CHARACTERS

GENERAL LEW WALLACE....................President of the Court
CAPTAIN WILLIAMS.................Union Officer in charge of Old
　　　　　　　　　　　　　　　　Capital Jail, Washington, D.C.
OTIS H. BAKER.................................Defense Counsel
LT. COL. N. P. CHIPMAN.....................The Judge Advocate
HENRY WIRZ....................................The Defendant
MAJOR D. HOSMER.....................Assistant Judge Advocate
LOUIS SCHADE.........................Assistant Defense Counsel
DR. C. M. FORD.......................Prison Surgeon at the Old
　　　　　　　　　　　　　　　　Capital Jail, Washington, D.C.
COURT CLERK

WITNESSES (In order of appearance)

LT. COL. CHANDLER.................................first witness
DR. JOHN C. BATES..............................second witness
AMBROSE SPENCER................................third witness
JAMES H. DAVIDSON..............................fourth witness
JASPER CULVER....................................fifth witness
JAMES W. GRAY....................................sixth witness

NON-SPEAKING PARTS

Three Union Soldiers and one Lieutenant
Court Reporter
Three newspapermen
Judges assisting General Wallace:
　　GENERAL MOTT
　　GENERAL THOMAS
　　GENERAL GEARY
　　GENERAL FESSENDEN
　　GENERAL BALLIER
　　COLONEL ALLCOCK
　　COLONEL STIBBS

SYNOPSIS

The action of the play takes place in the United States Court of Claims, Washington, D.C.
This courtroom was "borrowed" by The Military Commission to provide, in this unusual instance, space for the public.

ACT ONE

SCENE 1: A day in August, 1865.
SCENE 2: A week later.

ACT TWO

SCENE 1: The following morning.
SCENE 2: The next day.

DESCRIPTION OF MAIN CHARACTERS

GENERAL LEW WALLACE: He is President of the Court. As he speaks, he reveals a chill and remote authority. He is a Major General, thirty-seven years of age.

LT. COL. N. P. CHIPMAN (The Judge Advocate): He is thirty-one, a battle veteran whose youthful idealism has been hardened by war to a fierce unyielding partisanship. We must sense humane impulses held underneath a compulsion of bitterness toward the South— warring feelings creating a quality of controlled tension.

OTIS H. BAKER (Defense Counsel): He is in his forties; a lawyer of polish, experience, and daring; of an ironic, worldly intelligence. Method must be sensed in his every move—even when he appears most angry.

HENRY WIRZ (The Defendant): Dressed in shabby black clothes and a white shirt open at the throat, obviously not well, he still manages to suggest the bearing of a soldier. Arrogant, defiant, fatalistic, con-temptuous—a mixture of all these attitudes. He is in his forties.

LT. COL. CHANDLER: We should see him as a man of breeding and courage, caught through the questioning between loyalty to his de-feated cause and his essential humanity.

DR. JOHN C. BATES: He is a type of country doctor; an honest man with small vanities.

AMBROSE SPENCER: A somewhat glib, unctuous, coarse country squire type.

JAMES H. DAVIDSON: He is young. War and prison experience haunt his face. He is feeble and ill at ease, and his postwar motley costume of Army tunic and civilian trousers hangs loosely on his gaunt frame. One may imagine how deeply he longs for a quiet, restful place.

JASPER CULVER: There is a punch-drunk suggestion in his walk. He smiles uncertainly. He is sworn in. As he gets into his story, he will begin to act it out.

JAMES W. GRAY: He is a strong, tough-looking soldier—a type to bet on as the sole survivor of some desperate situation. He is dressed sharp, down to shiny cavalry boots.

THE ANDERSONVILLE TRIAL was first presented by William Darrid, Eleanore Saidenberg, and Daniel Hollywood at Henry Miller's Theatre, New York City, on December 29, 1959. It was directed by Jose Ferrer, and the production was designed and lighted by Will Steven Armstrong. The cast was as follows:

(In Order of Speaking)

GENERAL LEW WALLACE (President of the Court)......Russell Hardie
LIEUTENANT ....Robert Burr
COURT CLERK.............................Heywood Hale Broun
LT. COL. N. P. CHIPMAN (the Judge Advocate)......George C. Scott
OTIS H. BAKER (the Defense Counsel)................Albert Dekker
CAPTAIN WILLIAMS...............................Al Henderson
HENRY WIRZ (the Defendant)....................Herbert Berghof
LIEUTENANT COLONEL CHANDLER....................Robert Carroll
LOUIS SCHADE (Assistant Defense Counsel)..........James Arenton
DR. JOHN C. BATES.................................Ian Herrick
AMBROSE SPENCER..............................Moultrie Patten
DR. C. M. FORD (Prison Surgeon)..................Douglas Herrick
JAMES H. DAVIDSON..............................James Greene
MAJOR D. HOSMER (Assistant Judge Advocate)......Howard Wierum
JASPER CULVER................................Robert Gerringer
GEORGE W. GRAY................................Frank Sutton
UNION SOLDIERS..........Robert Downey, Martin West, Lou Frizzell
COURT REPORTER.............................Vincent Donahue
NEWSPAPERMEN......Robert Mayer, Richard Poston, William Scharf

GENERAL MOTT		Clifford Carpenter
GENERAL THOMAS		Taylor Graves
GENERAL GEARY		John Leslie
GENERAL FESSENDEN	ASSISTING JUDGES	Owen Pavitt
GENERAL BALLIER		William Hussung
COLONEL ALLCOCK		Archie Smith
COLONEL STIBBS		Freeman Meskimen

THE ANDERSONVILLE TRIAL

ACT I

SCENE 1

The Court of Claims, Washington, D.C. A morning in August, 1865. The atmosphere is sweltering. The room is furnished simply. A number of conference type tables arranged to form a courtroom area: defense and prosecution tables, R. and L., opposite sides, the judges' table, C., to the rear so that they will sit facing the audience, the witness chair, R. C., placed near the judges' table. Next to the defense table we note the bizarre element of a chaise longue, D. R. It is for the prisoner who is ill and who will recline through most of the trial. Two tall French windows are in R. wall. An American flag is mounted on the wall behind the judges' table. Mounted on a stand, above judges' is a table, a huge schematic drawing of the Andersonville stockade—a rectangle with a simple sketching in of elements such as a stream, walls, entrance gate, deadline, "hospital," burial ground, etc.

The doors are opened by two Union Soldiers. A Lieutenant in charge, gestures silently and forcefully, motioning the others to their locations in the room. Immediately following, government and defense counsel enter in the stream of court Personnel and Newspapermen, all moving to assigned tables. Nobody sits down. The entrance of the Judges is expected momentarily. The others have all gone to their places swiftly—all having been here before. The uniformed Prosecutors, (Judge Advocate and Assistant Judge Advocate), are Lt. Col. N. P. Chipman and

9

Major D. Hosmer. Opposite them are Otis H. Baker and Louis Schade, representing the defendant. Counsel confer rapidly at their separate tables. (The subject, as we shall learn in a moment, is the absence of the defendant.) Captain Williams now enters and strides over to Col. Chipman, to whom he speaks with an air of suppressed excitement. He breaks off almost as soon as he begins— as the Judges enter. All parties come to attention as the Judges, eight Union officers of rank in full uniform, take their places. They sit flanking General Lew Wallace, President of the Court. There is a quality of cold overriding power and purpose in control as proceedings start. As Wallace speaks, he reveals a chill and remote authority. He is a major general.

WALLACE. (*Banging gavel down once.*) This military court convened by order of the War Department is now in session. The lieutenant in charge is advised to post additional guards in the corridor. A lane must be kept clear at all times to the courtroom doors.

LIEUTENANT. Yes, sir. (*He goes out.*)

WALLACE. Have all witnesses listed to appear in these proceedings reported to the clerk of the Court?

CLERK. All have reported to the clerk, sir, and are on hand.

WALLACE. I take it all concerned with these proceedings have signed the necessary oath of allegiance to the government of the United States.

CLERK. Yes, sir. (*Lieutenant re-enters, takes up post at closed doors.*)

WALLACE. (*As he refers to counsel by name, they acknowledge by a nod.*) Lt. Col. N. P. Chipman, for the War Department. Mr. Otis Baker for the defense. The defendant, Henry Wirz, is to be tried by this military commission consisting of —— (*Glancing down the line of the Judges.*) General Mott . . . General Thomas . . . General Geary . . . General Fessenden . . . General Ballier . . . Colonel Allcock . . . Colonel Stibbs . . . and myself, General Wallace. Has the defense any objection to any of its members?

BAKER. No objection.

WALLACE. I do not see the defendant.

10

CHIPMAN. If the Court please, Captain Williams is here and will explain his absence. (*Captain Williams forward.*)

WILLIAMS. Sir, regarding the defendant. He will be brought here shortly.

WALLACE. Is he ill?

WILLIAMS. (*Blurting it.*) Sir, he is temporarily indisposed, following his attempt on his life early this morning which was foiled by the alertness of the guards ——

WALLACE. Mr. Wirz attempted to take his life?

WILLIAMS. Unsuccessfully, sir.

WALLACE. Captain, you will explain to the Court how such an attempt could have possibly occurred.

WILLIAMS. Sir, Mr. Wirz tried to slash his wrist after breaking a bottle.

WALLACE. A bottle?

WILLIAMS. A brandy bottle which he receives daily as a stimulant by order of Dr. Ford ——

WALLACE. The incident should not have occurred —— You are charged with custody of the prisoner. You will take the necessary steps so it will not occur again. You say the prisoner is in condition to appear shortly?

WILLIAMS. Within a few minutes, and I will personally ——

WALLACE. (*Cutting him off.*) That is all.

WILLIAMS. Yes sir. (*Exits, to re-enter later with Captain Wirz.*)

WALLACE. I will ask Defense counsel to plead to the indictment in the absence of the defendant.

BAKER. We would prefer, if the Court will permit, that Captain Wirz hear the charges against him directly ——

WALLACE. This trial has been postponed several times and the Court intends to proceed this morning without further delay. (*More command than question.*) Will counsel plead to the charge?

BAKER. Counsel will plead.

WALLACE. If the judge advocate is ready.

CHIPMAN. Ready, sir.

WALLACE. The indictment will be read. (*Chipman's movement reflects something of the man at once—an angry aggressive quality. He is 32, a battle veteran. Essentially he is a man of willful personal independence who endures the yoke of discipline with difficulty. He communicates an intense anger under control as he reads the indictment.*)

11

CHIPMAN. (*Seated.*) Charge—Criminal conspiracy to destroy the lives of soldiers of the United States in violation of the laws and customs of war.

Specification—That Henry Wirz who was in charge of the Confederate Prison at Andersonville, Georgia, did keep in barbarously close confinement federal soldiers, up to the number of forty thousand, without adequate shelter against the burning heat of summer or the cold of winter and—

Specification—That said Henry Wirz in carrying out this conspiracy did not provide the prisoners of war with sufficient food, clothing or medical care, causing them to languish and die to the number of more than fourteen thousand.

Specification—That he established a line known as the "Deadline" and that he instructed the prison guards stationed on the walls of the prison stockade to fire upon and kill any prisoner who might pass beyond that deadline.

Specification—That he used bloodhounds to hunt down, seize and mangle escaping prisoners of war, through these various causes bringing about the deaths of about fifty federal soldiers, their names unknown.

Specification—That through direct order and/or by his own hand he brought about the murder of thirteen prisoners, their names unknown.

WALLACE. Mr. Baker, pleading for the prisoner—how do you plead to the charge?

BAKER. (*Seated. Making his objection speedily, aware that they are all going to be rejected.*) We interpose a motion—that this military court discharge itself as being without proper jurisdiction now that the war is over.

CHIPMAN. This court has jurisdiction under the war powers of the President, which are still in force. It is well known that die-hard rebel officers still refuse to lay down their arms. Officially and in fact the war continues. Move to deny.

WALLACE. The motion is denied.

BAKER. Motion to postpone . . . on the ground that potential witnesses who in more normal times might speak for the defendant refuse to do so now, for fear their motives will be misunderstood as signifying support of the late Confederacy.

CHIPMAN. (*With open sarcasm.*) If Mr. Baker's witnesses can in good conscience take the oath of loyalty to the government of the United States, they have nothing to fear.

BAKER. The Court is aware of the temper of the times. It is only four short months since Mr. Lincoln was assassinated.

WALLACE. (*A clap of thunder.*) We will leave that name out of this trial!

BAKER. (*Rises.*) Nevertheless, Mr. Lincoln's presence is in this room—his murder is felt in this room—and it swells the charge of murder against the defendant to gigantic size ——

CHIPMAN. For which the Southern cause is responsible. And counsel will not turn Mr. Lincoln's tragic death to his advantage here.

BAKER. It is my general concern, sir, that the indictment leaves out Captain Wirz' military superiors, making him the single target of the national mood of vengeance against the South ——

WALLACE. (*Gavel.*) That will be all, Mr. Baker. Motion denied. If you have no further motions ——

BAKER. I do. As to the specifications alleging the crime of murder and abetting murder against certain persons, move to strike them since no persons are named.

CHIPMAN. (*Rise, to* L. *of Generals.*) Counsel cannot with his motions dispose of the horror of 14,000 unknown dead dumped into unmarked graves at Andersonville. Better records were kept of bales of cotton. Move to deny.

BAKER. Will the Judge advocate tell us where accurate prison records were kept during the War? (*Chipman reacts with annoyance.*) The Judge Advocate owes me common courtesy here. A person accused of crimes punishable by death is entitled to a proper defense.

CHIPMAN. We know what is defended here. Counsel's political motives are well understood.

WALLACE. (*Raps gavel.*) The exchange will stop.

BAKER. I only remind the Judge Advocate that he is in a court of law, and no longer on the battlefield. He behaves as if the horror of war was not universal. The North had its Andersonvilles.

WALLACE. The government of the United States is not on trial here, Mr. Baker.

BAKER. That remains to be seen.

WALLACE. (*Rising.*) Mr. Baker ——!

BAKER. Meaning no offense to the court —— The remark stated

13

in full would have been . . . "That remains to be seen through the testimony that will be offered here." I was referring to what the record will show, sir . . .

WALLACE. The court is not misled —— (*The court door is opened from the outside by Capt. Williams who indicates to the Lieutenant in charge that the Prisoner is ready to appear.*) In the future you will exercise care in your remarks to this court, Mr. Baker. Motion denied.

LIEUTENANT. Prisoner to the court! (*Wirz enters, followed by Dr. Ford who carries his medical bag and who is followed by Capt. Williams. Ford and Williams go above witness chair to sit in reporters' area, front of windows. Wirz crosses toward couch, Baker indicates to him to wait, R. of witness chair.*)

WALLACE. (*To Baker.*) If you have no further motions, I will order the defendant to plead to the charge.

BAKER. No further motion, but if the court please, we have made a special request of the Judge Advocate on behalf of the defendant —which he has apparently forgotten.

CHIPMAN. (*Seated.*) It has been requested that the prisoner be permitted to recline on a sofa during the proceedings on his claim of great pain and weakness owing to a so-called war wound ——

WIRZ. (*He speaks with a slight Germanic accent.*) Not so-called, Colonel. I was a soldier in the line. I was honorably wounded at the Battle of Seven Pines, and ——

CHIPMAN. The defendant is not the only man in this room who bears the scars of war.

WIRZ. I will not be slandered.

WALLACE. Permission is granted for the prisoner to recline during the proceedings, and he will now plead ——

WIRZ. (*Breaking in swiftly, speaking with heavy irony, he is still standing.*) I thank you, General. I wish to make a statement, sir, as to my ——

WALLACE. You will have an opportunity to do so ——

WIRZ. (*Finishing.*) —as to my attempt on my own life this morning, if the Court is interested ——

WALLACE. Make your statement.

WIRZ. It was not guilt of conscience that drove me to that act. I have no guilt of conscience. None whatsoever ——

WALLACE. If that is all you have to say ——

WIRZ. Only a few words more, sir. I calmly sized up the situa-

14

tion, as a soldier. As I see it I have simply no chance whatsoever and I decided not to give the government the satisfaction ——
WALLACE. (Overlapping.) That will be all, Mr. Wirz.
WIRZ. One other matter, sir ——
WALLACE. That will be all!
WIRZ. Then the Court will not permit me to mention a personal matter that should be the concern of the Court?
WALLACE. You will speak to the point—what is it?
WIRZ. I write letters to my family and do not know if they are received.
WALLACE. The Court has nothing to do with the mails. Possibly your letters are delayed. Conditions are still unsettled.
WIRZ. General, I was taken from the midst of my family without warning and under the eyes of my children arrested. I do not care what the newspapers call me—let them call me the butcher of Andersonville. But what my children think of their father—that is important to me. I have a right to present myself as I wish to my children. *I have that right.* It is a cruelty that I do not know if my letters are received. (General Thomas whispers to Wallace.)
WALLACE. If you wish, we will see to it that your letters go by military packet to your home ——
WIRZ. (Appearing to fawn, but with irony.) I thank the Court most kindly. They have been most considerate to me. The medical care, the spiritual comfort of the priest who is permitted to visit me daily in my cell. The Court has been most kind. (With sudden venom.) All that is wanted of me is my life. I am not fooled!
BAKER. (Crosses to Wirz—takes him to couch—crosses up to General's table.) Will the Court make due allowance for the strain the defendant is under ——?
CHIPMAN. (Overlapping.) Defense counsel must share guilt with the prisoner for that outburst ——
(As Chipman and Baker now quarrel, Wallace remains stonily silent.)
BAKER. (Crosses to R. C. Overlapping.) Everything is conspiracy in the eyes of the Judge Advocate —— I'm not here to help you make your case—much as you would like ——
CHIPMAN. (Rises, crosses to L. C.) I would like you to be still now ——
BAKER. (Overlapping.) And I remind you—that normal courtroom behavior ——

CHIPMAN. Nothing is normal here, sir ——

BAKER. —that normal courtroom behavior calls for the outward appearance—I don't care what you *think*—that one's opponent is acting in good faith ——

CHIPMAN. Which I cannot assume, sir, since I know where you stand ——

BAKER. And where is that, Colonel?

CHIPMAN. On the side of those who secretly opposed this government when it was fighting for its life. Who pays you here?

BAKER. Not the government.

CHIPMAN. No, not this government but the remnants of that other—still active. (*Crosses* L. *to chair, sits.*)

BAKER. Make a political accusation against a man and nothing he says will be considered for its own sake. The Judge Advocate is suspicious of my politics and wants to know who pays me. (*Glancing toward Chipman.*) If the Court please, I'll oblige the Judge Advocate. (*Wallace remains furiously silent. Baker crosses to Chipman.*) I am paid by a committee formed to defend Capt. Wirz. I am not involved in this case in the way the Judge Advocate would wish. I take my cases where I find them, subject to one condition— I must feel there's a shade—the smallest shade of doubt—as to a man's guilt. (*Crosses to* R. *of witness chair.*) Regarding my politics in my home city of Baltimore, a city of divided loyalties, some held that I was an enemy to the Confederate side because I felt that slavery was not worth dying for since it was an unworkable institution that was doomed to extinction anyway. And there were the others who suspected me because I was lukewarm on the glorious future that would follow a Northern victory. The Colonel might make his own position clearer.

CHIPMAN. (*Seated.*) I will try to do that, Mr. Baker. I was brought up to believe that slavery was evil. I answered Mr. Lincoln's second call for volunteers because it was natural for me to go to war against a cause which wished to perpetuate human bondage. I am here in the service of the Union to secure justice for men barbarously murdered by that Southern cause. I am personally involved here, Mr. Baker, if you are not ——

BAKER. As a lawyer or as a clerk under orders to process Wirz through to the hangman? (*Chipman rises, is restrained by Hosmer and sits—Baker crosses to chair,* R., *speaks to Schade.*) As I thought. We can make the bull charge. (*Sits.*)

WALLACE. (*After a long silence speaks in a flatly powerful* tone.) I take it gentlemen are through. Under military law we could of course dispense with defense counsel; the defendant would not have to be present. And this case could be heard in a small room. But the government has seen fit to set it here in the Court of Claims and before an audience. Conceding the temper of the times and the emotions of all parties, we intend to hold this trial within bounds. I do not advise further testing the power of the Court to maintain order . . . (Briskly.) Defense counsel has stated he has no further motions and I will now order the defendant to plead to the charge. Prisoner, how do you plead?

BAKER. The prisoner enters a plea of not guilty to the charge and all specifications.

WALLACE. The Judge Advocate will summon his first witness. (As Chipman begins, Wirz beckons to Baker.)

CHIPMAN. On the general charge of criminal conspiracy, we summon Mr. D. T. Chandler. (In the time it takes for Chandler's name to be bawled into the witness room, for Chandler to appear, walk to the witness chair, and be sworn, we hear the exchange at the defense table.)

WIRZ. Baker, you have all the necessary documents ——

GUARD. (Calls off.) Mr. D. T. Chandler!

BAKER. Yes.

WIRZ. And the evidence that I released the youngest Northern prisoners on parole—you remember how I let them out to pick blackberries —— (Chandler enters—crosses to Clerk, R.)

BAKER. I know. (Chandler sworn in by Clerk.)

WIRZ. (Pause.) But it will do no good. (The tone is cryptic.) I must die . . . Yes . . . I must die . . . (Pause.) The real crime I have committed, Baker—you understand what it is of course.

BAKER. Well?

WIRZ. That I chose the losing side.

CHIPMAN. Before we begin we will state briefly the rule of evidence applying in cases of criminal conspiracy. The evidence of a common design to commit a criminal act is sufficient to convict— and we shall prove that such a common design existed at Andersonville—to which the defendant willingly lent himself. (General Wallace indicates that Chipman may start interrogation. We should see Chandler as a man of breeding and courage, caught through the questioning between loyalty to his defeated cause and

17

his essential humanity.) Mr. Chandler, please state how you were employed during the year 1864.

CHANDLER. I served in the Army of the Confederacy, with the rank of lieutenant colonel.

CHIPMAN. What was your official duty?

CHANDLER. I was assigned by the war office to inspect and report on the military prisons maintained by the Confederacy.

CHIPMAN. Did you, in the course of an official assignment, go to the Andersonville military prison situated in Sumter County, Georgia?

CHANDLER. Yes, sir. There had been civilian complaints forwarded to Richmond.

CHIPMAN. How long did you remain at Andersonville?

CHANDLER. Two weeks.

CHIPMAN. (*Rises—crosses above Generals' table. Pointing to the chart, with pointer.*) I ask you if that is a fair map of the Andersonville stockade?

CHANDLER. Yes, it is.

CHIPMAN. Will you state the dimensions of the stockade—its area?

CHANDLER. A thousand feet on the longer side, from north to south. 800 feet from east to west, covering about sixteen acres of ground.

CHIPMAN. (*Crosses to table, L.*) What was the nature of the terrain?

CHANDLER. Simply earth—bare ground.

CHIPMAN. Was that the condition of the terrain in advance of it being selected as a site for the camp?

CHANDLER. No, sir. The tract was originally part of a section of pine woods.

CHIPMAN. And what can you tell us of the climate in that part of Georgia? I refer now to extremes of temperature. Of summer heat and winter cold.

CHANDLER. In July and August it would be quite high, at times over a hundred degrees. Winters, it could be near freezing and rainy.

CHIPMAN. Was that camp laid out with provision for shelter of any kind?

CHANDLER. No, sir.

CHIPMAN. (*Crosses above Generals to map.*) This outer stockade wall—describe it, sir.

18

CHANDLER. A wall some fifteen to twenty feet high, consisting of rough-hewn timbers. A platform ran along the top of the wall and at regular intervals there were sentry boxes.

CHIPMAN. This line inside the wall ——

CHANDLER. That was a line of posts running parallel to the outer wall—about twenty-five feet inside it.

CHIPMAN. It had a name, did it not?

CHANDLER. The "dead-line"—so called because a prisoner going beyond it could be shot by the guard.

CHIPMAN. This meandering line?

CHANDLER. That would be the stream that ran through the camp, entering under the wall on the west . . . and emerging under the east wall of the stockade.

CHIPMAN. Its width and depth?

CHANDLER. No more than a yard wide and perhaps a foot in depth. (Chipman points to map area.) The marshy area around the stream.

CHIPMAN. That marshy area could better be called swamp, could it not?

CHANDLER. Yes, sir; swamp.

CHIPMAN. Of what size?

CHANDLER. Extending about a hundred and fifty feet on either side of the stream.

CHIPMAN. And having a considerable oozy depth, did it not?

CHANDLER. Anyone venturing across it would probably sink to his waist . . . (Following the pointer.) That would be the cook-house . . . The burial trenches . . . The dead house . . . The main entrance gate ——

CHIPMAN. (Crosses to table, L. Sits.) Now, sir, as to the history of the camp. Will you state the circumstances under which it was established?

CHANDLER. By the latter part of '63 our prisoner-of-war camps were overcrowded. The War Office then decided to create a new camp.

CHIPMAN. Who was responsible for the establishment of this camp?

CHANDLER. General John H. Winder.

CHIPMAN. Now deceased?

CHANDLER. Yes.

CHIPMAN. And what was his official function?

CHANDLER. He was in charge of all military prisons for the Confederacy, east of the Mississippi.

CHIPMAN. You have said the tract of land on which the camp was located was originally part of a section of pine woods. The cutting down of every tree that might have provided shade—was Winder responsible for that?

CHANDLER. Yes, sir.

CHIPMAN. And this site—and the arrangements made for the care of the prisoners was known to and approved by the War Office?

CHANDLER. (*Tightly.*) I cannot say how much knowledge or approval. The Colonel knows how a line of command operates.

CHIPMAN. (*Rises—moves to witness—crosses to above Generals. With a burst.*) Wasn't it their responsibility ——? Withdrawn for the time being. Will you now describe conditions in the prison at Andersonville as you observed them?

CHANDLER. The area was tightly crowded with men when I inspected it.

CHIPMAN. Giving each prisoner—how much room, would you say?

CHANDLER. (*Crosses to table* L.) Thirty-five and a half square feet per prisoner.

CHIPMAN. A space equivalent to a cell only six feet on each side. What else did you find at Andersonville?

CHANDLER. (*Tightly.*) There was a general insufficiency—of water, shelter, and food. I think that would cover it.

CHIPMAN. (*Crosses to witness, his intensity is palpable.*) I think not. When you say an insufficiency of water you mean that the available water supply for all purposes—for drinking, washing, cooking—all came from that narrow brook, is that correct?

CHANDLER. Yes, sir.

CHIPMAN. And that stream was at the same time the repository for all the waste matter at the camp, was it not?

CHANDLER. Yes, sir.

CHIPMAN. All waste was emptied into that stream; the waste from the cookhouse and the bodily waste of the prisoners?

CHANDLER. Yes, sir.

CHIPMAN. Making that stream into a foul, sluggish sink, isn't that so?

CHANDLER. Yes ——

CHIPMAN. (*Crosses back of witness to* L.) And that foul, stinking stream a few feet wide was the water supply for forty thousand men, and that is what you meant by an insufficiency of water, isn't it?

CHANDLER. Yes.

CHIPMAN. (*Crosses to table* L.) And as to the insufficiency of shelter, there was in fact *no* shelter and the men lived on bare ground winter and summer or dug themselves into the ground, into borrows—is *that* correct?

CHANDLER. Yes, sir.

CHIPMAN. And as to the sort of clothing they had. You will please be specific, sir.

CHANDLER. (*More and more uneasy.*) *Some* wore shirts and trousers ——

CHIPMAN. *Some.* You mean the newly arrived prisoners *still* had their shirts and trousers, don't you?

CHANDLER. Yes.

CHIPMAN. You mean the rest, the vast number of them, were in rags, don't you?

CHANDLER. Yes.

CHIPMAN. You mean those men were simply in a state of nakedness and near nakedness under the terrible weather conditions you described a moment ago—isn't that so?

CHANDLER. Yes.

CHIPMAN. (*Crosses to front of Generals.*) And the food?·

CHANDLER. Mostly corn meal.

CHIPMAN. Ground fine or coarse?

CHANDLER. Unbolted meal.

CHIPMAN. Unbolted meal. Meaning meal ground so coarse it was as good as swallowing a knife for what it did to a man's insides considering the weakened condition those men were in. Isn't that so, Mr. Chandler?

CHANDLER. Yes, sir.

CHIPMAN. Did the men ever get anything else to eat outside of this meal?

CHANDLER. A bit of meat now and then.

CHIPMAN. What sort of meat?

CHANDLER. Not very good.

CHIPMAN. (*Moves to Chandler.*) Not very good. The prisoners had a joke about that meat, didn't they? A grim kind of a soldier

21

joke to describe that meat from sick, dying mules and horses. They told you that the animal that meat came from—it had to be held up on its legs to be slaughtered—didn't they?

CHANDLER. Jokes of that sort—yes.

CHIPMAN. (*Crosses behind witness to* R.) And you saw with your own eyes it was rotten, maggot-ridden meat, and that is what you meant when you said it wasn't very good, didn't you?

CHANDLER. Yes ——

CHIPMAN. And the conditions they were living under drove them to extreme measures in the effort to survive, isn't that so?

CHANDLER. Extreme—yes, sir.

CHIPMAN. (*Paces front of Generals.*) To the point where they regarded rats as a delicacy, isn't that so?

CHANDLER. Yes, sir.

CHIPMAN. To the point that when one of them died, the others, in the desperation they had been driven to, stripped his body clean of whatever was on it in five minutes—of boots or trousers if he had any, or bread, or greenbacks to bribe the guards—anything that might help them stay alive—isn't that correct?

CHANDLER. Yes, sir.

CHIPMAN. (L. *of witness.*) Driven in their desperation to the point of cannibalism, isn't that so?

CHANDLER. Yes ——

CHIPMAN. You were able to establish that in your mind for a fact?

CHANDLER. Yes.

CHIPMAN. (*Moves to* R. *of Chandler.*) How? (*As Chandler hesitates.*) As delicately as you wish, Mr. Chandler.

CHANDLER. (*After a moment, with difficulty.*) Well—by the condition of some bodies—very rough surgery had been performed.

CHIPMAN. And so, in that place, men had been driven to the disposition of beasts ——

CHANDLER. Yes.

CHIPMAN. (*Crosses up to map.*) And if I were now to sum up Andersonville as a pit—an animal pit in which men wallowed—the sick, the dying, the insane wallowing among the dead—would I exaggerate the picture of that place?

CHANDLER. No.

CHIPMAN. (*Crosses above Generals to table,* L.) Concerning

what you saw there . . . you submitted a report with recommendations to General Winder and your War Office, did you not?
CHANDLER. I did.
CHIPMAN. (*Handing over a document to Chandler.*) This is a copy of that report?
CHANDLER. (*Glancing at it and handing it back.*) That is the report.
CHIPMAN. Offered in evidence. (*Presents report to Wallace who returns it to him.*) You say in this report that Andersonville is a blot on the Confederacy. You recommend that all prisoners be transferred to other prisons without delay and that Andersonville be immediately closed down.
CHANDLER. I did; yes. (*Chipman hands report to Court Clerk.*)
COURT CLERK. Exhibit One, for the Government.
CHIPMAN. (*Crosses to table, L.*) And that report was ignored, was it not? Ignored, disregarded, the condition allowed to continue ———?
CHANDLER. Colonel, I am not here to indict the leaders of the cause for which I fought, as plotting the murder of defenseless men.
CHIPMAN. (*Crosses to front of Generals' table.*) The report revealing how Winder and Wirz were operating that camp was ignored ———
CHANDLER. I have told you I could not endure Andersonville. You people act as though you were better human beings than we were!
CHIPMAN. No, but our cause was. Your report was ignored?
CHANDLER. Due to the crisis—the bitterness—the disorder—with General Sherman marching through Georgia burning his way ———
CHIPMAN. It was ignored ———?
CHANDLER. As your officers would have ignored it, sir, if it had been General Lee marching through Pennsylvania into New York!
WALLACE. Mr. Chandler ———
CHANDLER. This situation is difficult for me. (*Chipman crosses to table, L.*)
WALLACE. (*Stern, but not hard, he respects Chandler.*) Nevertheless, you must answer the question. The Judge Advocate will repeat the question and you *will* answer it.

CHIPMAN. Your report on Andersonville was ignored, was it not?

CHANDLER. Yes, sir.

CHIPMAN. Did General Winder ever express to you his disposition toward those prisoners?

CHANDLER. When I spoke to General Winder he had hard and bitter feelings toward them.

CHIPMAN. And how did he express those feelings?

CHANDLER. He finally said that if half of the prisoners died, there would then be twice as much room for the rest ——

CHIPMAN. And the half slated for the grave were well on their way at Andersonville, weren't they? (*Crosses above witness to* R.) Mr. Wirz set up certain rules for that camp, rules relative to punishing prisoners attempting to escape ——?

CHANDLER. Yes, sir.

CHIPMAN. His command of that camp conforming to Winder's inhuman disposition toward those men?

BAKER. I must ask the Judge Advocate what he means by that suggestive, ambiguous phrase, *conforming to*.

CHIPMAN. Withdrawn. Those rules Mr. Wirz set up at Andersonville—were they rules violating the customs of war?

CHANDLER. Well—yes.

CHIPMAN. Were they, in addition, cruel and inhuman rules?

CHANDLER. Yes.

CHIPMAN. Was Wirz the personal choice of Winder for superintendent of that camp?

CHANDLER. Yes.

CHIPMAN. That will be all. (*Crosses to table*, L., *sits.*)

BAKER. Col. Chandler, you made a second report on Andersonville to the Confederate war office, did you not?

CHANDLER. I did, yes sir.

BAKER. This is a copy of that report? (*He hands the report to Schade, who shows it to Chandler.*)

CHANDLER. (*Scrutinizing it briefly and handing it back to Schade.*) It is.

SCHADE. (*Shows report to Wallace.*) Submitted for the Defense —Entered in evidence. (*Gives report to Clerk.*)

CLERK. Exhibit number one for the Defense.

BAKER. In this report—to which the judge Advocate has failed to

24

call attention—you recommend the dismissal of General Winder.

CHANDLER. Yes.

BAKER. But *not* of Capt. Wirz.

CHANDLER. No.

BAKER. Why not?

CHANDLER. At the time I inspected Andersonville, I saw nothing in Capt. Wirz' conduct of a malignant disposition toward those men, that would have justified asking for his dismissal.

BAKER. I note in the same report that you took various prisoners aside, urging them to speak freely as to any instance of ill treatment by Captain Wirz—and they had no complaints on that score?

CHANDLER. No, sir.

BAKER. In other words, neither you nor the prisoners, who were presumably being subjected to Capt. Wirz' cruel and inhuman treatment blamed him for it, did you?

CHANDLER. No, sir.

BAKER. No more questions. Thank you, sir.

CHIPMAN. (*Seated.*) Mr. Chandler, very often, as you know, commanders are forewarned of inspection and dress up their commands in advance. Couldn't that have occurred in your case?

CHANDLER. Possibly.

CHIPMAN. And isn't it possible that they would fear the consequences of complaints against Wirz? Those men did not know you, and Wirz would still be in command after you were gone. And under those circumstances, isn't it very possible that they would not answer you truthfully?

CHANDLER. Perhaps. I did the best I could with that Andersonville situation ——

CHIPMAN. (*Inwardly raging, silent for a moment.*) Did Wirz do the best he could? (*Rises—crosses to witness.*) In spite of Winder's orders, couldn't he have chosen to . . . (*Frustrated.*) . . . there are ways!

BAKER. Ways of doing what? Evading the orders of his superior? What is the Judge Advocate suggesting?

CHIPMAN. (*Crosses to table, L., sits.*) Withdrawn. That will be all, thank you, Mr. Chandler.

WALLACE. If there are no other questions the witness may step down. The Court thanks the witness. (*Chandler goes. Chipman's tone is becoming more peremptory.*)

CHIPMAN. We call Dr. John C. Bates to the stand.

LIEUTENANT. Dr. John C. Bates. (*Bates comes in and is sworn.*)

CHIPMAN. (*Seated.*) Dr. Bates, were you in the service of the Confederate Army during the year 1864?

BATES. Yes, sir.

CHIPMAN. Were you at any time inside the Andersonville stockade?

BATES. Yes, sir. For about eight months during '64.

CHIPMAN. In what capacity were you there?

BATES. As a medical officer—assigned to the camp by the Surgeon General. I can't say I asked for it.

CHIPMAN. I suppose not. Describe your activity there as a physician.

BATES. Writing prescriptions for drugs that were not available, amputations of limbs due to gangrene—quite a lot of that—and certifying the dead in my section each morning—quite a lot of that too.

CHIPMAN. Did you in the course of your stay there make any estimate of the rate of death at that place?

BATES. I did; yes, sir. I had always kept a ledger book covering the ailments and treatment of my patients in civil life—farmers— their families—their horses too. And I decided to keep some sort of a record in that camp . . . because I was deeply shocked by that place when I came there.

CHIPMAN. Please tell the Court what your estimate of the death rate was.

BATES. In the spring months it averaged fifty, sixty, seventy men a day . . . in spells of extreme heat during the summer reaching a hundred men a day. More in May than in April, more in June than in May, and in July, August, September, three thousand men a month were dying.

CHIPMAN. What were the principal causes for that high rate of death?

BATES. The lack of sanitary facilities—the lack of exercise—the anemia of the men from lack of food rendering them subject to fatal illness from the slightest abrasion or infection—the lack of medical supplies.

CHIPMAN. And, Dr. Bates, in your professional opinion, how

many of the thousands who died there would have lived if conditions had at least been sanitary?

BATES. I would estimate—seventy-five to eighty per cent.

CHIPMAN. Ten to eleven thousand of those fourteen thousand men ——

BATES. Yes, sir.

CHIPMAN. Can you think of sanitary measures which, if taken at Andersonville, would have saved lives ——?

BATES. A number; yes.

CHIPMAN. (*Rises—crosses to front of Generals.*) Were such measures suggested to Wirz?

BATES. Yes, sir. By myself—perhaps others.

CHIPMAN. And what did he say?

BATES. He said I was a doctor and didn't understand his difficulties running a huge camp like that. He was downright incoherent—damned me for a Yankee sympathizer—and cursed me out in English, German and some other foreign dialect ——

WIRZ. French. That was French, Dr. Bates ——

BATES. French, eh? (*Chipman crosses to table, L.*)

WALLACE. (*Brings down gavel, frowning at Wirz.*) For your own good, Mr. Wirz, keep in mind that your situation here is not amusing.

WIRZ. No, sir—and I can't explain it to myself or to the Court, why I have this feeling to laugh, hearing how I killed all those men. Perhaps the Court can explain it.

WALLACE. Do not play the clown here. . . . Continue, Colonel.

CHIPMAN. Only one more question—on that not so humorous occasion when you spoke to Mr. Wirz and he complained to you that his job was difficult . . . did you understand him to mean his job was difficult administratively or difficult— (*Searching for his thought*)—humanly?

BATES. Mr. Wirz dwelt on *his* difficulties—not the men's.

CHIPMAN. That will be all, Doctor. Thank you. (*Sits.*)

BAKER. Dr. Bates, you regard yourself as a fair-minded man, don't you?

BATES. I do.

BAKER. The fact that you dislike Captain Wirz has not influenced your testimony here in any way, has it?

BATES. No, it has not ——

BAKER. But you *did* dislike him, didn't you?

BATES. Not so as to influence my professional objective judgment ——

BAKER. I now address myself to the professional *objective* side of you, Doctor—strictly to that side. So far as you know, by whose authority was the amount of food per prisoner decided on?

BATES. By the Commissary General at Richmond, I believe.

BAKER. And not by Captain Wirz. And by whose authority was the amount and type of medical supply to the camp decided on?

BATES. Surgeon General.

BAKER. And not by Captain Wirz. He was responsible neither for the lack of food nor the inadequate medical supplies.

BATES. I would have to agree.

BAKER. You would have to agree. You don't want to agree but you would have to agree, is that what you mean, Dr. Bates? You seem to have found Captain Wirz rather calloused toward the condition of the prisoners.

BATES. This was my honest impression.

BAKER. Well, we are all entitled to our honest impressions. I recall you saying a few minutes ago that you were shocked at the high rate of death in the Andersonville prison when you came there.

BATES. Deeply shocked.

BAKER. (*With a show of sympathy.*) One can understand how unnerving it must have been. That was in what month by the way?

BATES. In February.

BAKER. And you had to face that unnerving scene day after day and month after month—it's difficult to understand how you could do that.

BATES. Well, sir, I had to steel myself and gradually the shock of it became endurable.

BAKER. I'm curious, Doctor—how gradually did your feeling of shock lessen? For example, how did you react to the dying—by June, let us say?

BATES. Not as much.

BAKER. And by September?

BATES. Far less ——

BAKER. So that by September, when, as you said, three thousand men a month were dying, you hardly reacted at all ——?

BATES. I meant—I had grown accustomed ——

BAKER. Of course you had. Any human being to save his sanity would have had to do that. (*Gesturing in direction of Wirz.*) So

28

Captain Wirz' "callousness" in that place wasn't so strange after all, was it?

BATES. (*Rattled.*) Well—my impression of Mr. Wirz remains the same, despite that.

BAKER. Thank you, that will be all. (*Baker back; Chipman forward—in a temper.*)

CHIPMAN. Dr. Bates, do you remember one single instance, in conversing with Wirz, when he expressed any criticism of the orders or disposition of his superior?

BAKER. Objection. I find that a strange question to be asked by a counsel for the War Department, himself a soldier. Is it being held against Captain Wirz that he did not make a public judgment of the motives of his military superior?

WALLACE. (*Considering.*) The Court must agree Wirz was not bound to comment on the orders of his military superior.

CHIPMAN. (*Crosses to L. of Generals. Hard.*) If the Court please, we are concerned here with the frame of mind of a man carrying out his superior's inhuman design. We are bound to explore his thinking when he obeyed those orders ——

BAKER. (*Rises.*) His thinking when he obeyed those orders? And if he did not like those orders what was he supposed to do? Disobey them? If conscience is the measure by which soldiers obey or disobey orders, one can hardly condemn the Army officers who went over to the Confederacy, since they did so on the ground of conscience —— (*The gavel comes down.*) And on that ground Robert E. Lee deserves a monument ——

WALLACE. (*Obviously perturbed.*) That will be all, Mr. Baker. . . . (*To Chipman.*) I am certain it was not in the mind of the Judge Advocate to raise the issue of disobedience to a superior officer ——

CHIPMAN. (*Crosses slowly to table, L., sits, inwardly resisting the Court.*) Under certain circumstances that issue may require consideration ——

WALLACE. (*With great deliberation—cueing, ordering and warning Chipman at the same time.*) The Court is not, of course, suggesting the line of inquiry the Judge Advocate is to take here. But the Court will say that it is disposed to draw its own inference as to a criminal design from evidence of the defendant's words and acts—and not from an examination of moral factors which can drop us into a bottomless pool of philosophic debate . . . I am certain the Judge Advocate will agree and that he will withdraw that question as to whether or not Wirz criticized his superior officer.

CHIPMAN. *(His glance travels sullenly down the line of Judges and then—flatly—)* The question is withdrawn. *(Rises—crosses front—to* R. *of witness. Openly furious now.)* Dr. Bates, you never grew so accustomed to that place as to forget your human obligation to those men, did you? You made it your daily business to bring in food from the outside for those starving men, didn't you?

BATES. Of course.

CHIPMAN. And there was plenty of food in the region of Andersonville to draw from, if Wirz had wished to bring it in—the yield of grain and vegetables in the region was considerable, wasn't it?

BAKER. Is Dr. Bates put forward as qualified to testify on the agricultural situation?

CHIPMAN. *(Crosses to table* L.*)* Withdrawn! If the Court please we wish to change the order of appearance of witnesses. We would like at this time to call a witness qualified to speak with accuracy on the available food supply in the vicinity of Andersonville.

WALLACE. Does defense counsel offer objection to a change in the order of the government witnesses?

BAKER. Not at all.

CHIPMAN. Ambrose Spencer to the stand.

WALLACE. The Court thanks you, Dr. Bates. You may step down.

LIEUTENANT. Ambrose Spencer!

BAKER. *(Cool and amused—pointing up Chipman's failure to thank the witness.)* We thank the witness.

CHIPMAN. Thank you, Dr. Bates! *(Bates exits. Spencer enters, is sworn in and takes the stand. Chipman's questioning is quick and impatient.)* Mr. Spencer, tell us where you reside.

SPENCER. I reside in the town of Americus, in Sumpter County, Georgia.

CHIPMAN. And your occupation?

SPENCER. I operate a plantation in that county—corn, cotton, tobacco, and ——

CHIPMAN. Is that plantation in proximity to the site of Andersonville?

SPENCER. Practically bordering it.

CHIPMAN. *(Paces—front of Generals.)* You are therefore in a position to know as well as any man the yield of grain and vegetables in the region of Andersonville.

SPENCER. I would say so.

CHIPMAN. How would you estimate yields for the years 1863 and 1864?

SPENCER. (*With obvious satisfaction.*) Both good years. Sumter and the adjoining county, Macon, I may point out, are part of a very productive area—sometimes termed the garden of the Confederacy, and ——

CHIPMAN. Yes, yes. We will have some details as to the yield.

SPENCER. Corn averaged about eight bushels to the acre, wheat six. That is the general average but we have land in Sumter county producing thirty-five ——

CHIPMAN. And as to vegetables?

SPENCER. We had an uncommon amount during the war since there was so little cotton planted and all the ground was pretty well planted in provisions.

CHIPMAN. (*Crosses to L. of Spencer.*) And, if Mr. Wirz had solicited food for the prisoners from the farms and plantations in the area—what in your judgment would have happened?

SPENCER. He would have gotten it. (*As Spencer goes on, Wirz sits up. Baker restrains him.*)

CHIPMAN. What makes you so certain of that?

SPENCER. The proof, sir, is that without it being solicited, there were people in the vicinity who came forward and made an effort to get food into that camp. In one case a group of women in Americus, including my wife, made that attempt.

CHIPMAN. (*Crosses to table, L., sits.*) Tell the Court what happened on that occasion.

SPENCER. Well, sir, the ladies thought it would be the Christian thing to do, having heard that the prisoners were doing so poorly. They obtained enough food through contributions to fill four wagons and had them driven ——

CHIPMAN. How large were those wagons?

SPENCER. The largest farm wagons they could find—each requiring four to six horses to pull it.

CHIPMAN. Making a load of how much food for those men?

SPENCER. Oh, maybe twenty tons.

CHIPMAN. Continue, sir.

SPENCER. They had those wagons driven up to the gate of the

stockade. Mr. Wirz was at the gate when those ladies arrived. He would not permit the food to be brought in —— He cursed those women. He told them they were giving aid and comfort to the enemy—that Yankee soldiers were unlawfully invading— looting the South—that those women were traitors—and worse. He used the violentest and profanest language I have ever heard in a man's mouth. He said if he had his way he would have a certain kind of a house built for those women and he would put them all in there where the Confederate soldiers would teach them loyalty in a hurry and teach it to them in a way they wouldn't forget ——

CHIPMAN. (Interrupting him.) We understand the remark, sir. And those ladies were turned away by Mr. Wirz from giving food to those starving men ——

SPENCER. They were turned away and they wept.

CHIPMAN. And if Mr. Wirz had solicited food—on Christian grounds and on behalf of the good name of the Confederacy—you think that would have brought in large amounts of food ——?

SPENCER. I am certain the people of Georgia would have responded ——

CHIPMAN. You were acquainted with the defendant, were you not?

SPENCER. Knew him quite well.

CHIPMAN. And you knew General Winder ——

SPENCER. Knew him too.

CHIPMAN. And from your knowledge, what can you tell us about the disposition of General Winder toward those prisoners?

SPENCER. When he came there once, Winder said that the Yankees had come South to take possession of the land and that he was endeavoring to satisfy them by giving them each a small plot—pointing to the gravesite.

CHIPMAN. And did you ever hear Wirz speak along the same lines?

SPENCER. I can tell you that he stated that he wished all those men in hell—that he boasted he was killing more Yankees at Andersonville than Lee was at Richmond ——

CHIPMAN. You heard those remarks ——?

SPENCER. Yes—to wipe out those men. That was the scheme.

CHIPMAN. Thank you. (He goes to table, L., sits.)

WIRZ. (As Chipman finishes.) That was my scheme, you say? To wipe out those men? On my head all those men? (He rises, Baker and Schade restrain him.)

32

WALLACE. (*Overlapping.*) Mr. Wirz . . . !
WIRZ. (*Breaks away—crosses up to Generals' table.*) I was a man
like other men ——
WALLACE. (*Overlapping.*) Counsel, you will restrain ——
WIRZ. Who will understand? An ordinary man like me—
assigned ——!
WALLACE. (*Overlapping.*) Guards! (*The two guards, Lieuten-
ant, Capt. Williams and Dr. Ford move in on Wirz.*)
WIRZ. (*Moves D. C.*) The drummer boys I saved—and now—I
am surrounded! (*The guards reach him as he slumps, faints. He
is carried to the sofa and all go back to their original positions
with only Dr. Ford staying by Wirz.*)
DR. FORD. (*To Schade.*) A bottle of brandy, in the bag.
BAKER. I ask for a postponement.
WALLACE. Dr. Ford?
FORD. (*Downstage of couch—He kneels.*) A fainting spell from
which he recovers. He lacks strength and suffers from strain but
should be well enough to continue—I suppose. (*Wirz comes to
consciousness, raising himself to lean on an elbow, watching.*)
WALLACE. This trial must go on ——
BAKER. If the Court please ——
WALLACE. It is no use, Mr. Baker ——
BAKER. The open bias of the witness is a case in point. I need
not remind the Court of the bitterness in our time ——
WALLACE. It is no use, Mr. Baker ——
BAKER. (*Crosses to Generals.*) Even the sight of a tattered
Confederate blouse is a cause for riot in the streets. The *very* air
is charged.
WALLACE. (*The case is beginning to coil about him.*) We are
not empowered to move this trial into the next century —— This
trial will continue. You will make clear to the defendant that
should there be another demonstration here he will be tried *in
absentia* —— (*Baker crosses to above couch.*)
WIRZ. *In absentia.* Latin for absence. I understand all languages
but the language of this trial —— (*Schade sits. Ford follows.*)
BAKER. The Court has suffered sufficient provocation to send
Capt. Wirz from this courtroom but I suggest it does not ——
WALLACE. (*In a cold deadly tone.*) You suggest we do not ——
BAKER. Since it is not he alone in this room who is stripped
down to naked hatred and anger ——
WALLACE. Counsel will cross-examine or stand down.

BAKER. Counsel will cross examine! Mr. Spencer, you don't regard yourself as prejudiced against Captain Wirz, do you?

SPENCER. I don't.

BAKER. Then why have you chosen to leave out of that touching tale about those women bringing food to that camp the fact that General Winder was there at the time and that it was he who ordered that food kept out?

SPENCER. Why?

BAKER. Yes, why. You were at the main gate of the camp together with other civilians and you heard General Winder say loudly and emphatically that that food was not to be brought in ——

SPENCER. Wirz wouldn't have tried in any case. I know that man.

BAKER. Answer the question—Why didn't you say so?

SPENCER. I wasn't asked.

BAKER. You weren't asked. Motion to dismiss Mr. Spencer's testimony as irrelevant in that it offers nothing other than that Captain Wirz was carrying out a direct order.

CHIPMAN. Move to deny!

BAKER. Will the Judge Advocate offer a ground for denial? Is he saying that Captain Wirz should have defied that direct order of General Winder's?

CHIPMAN. Will you deny that was an inhuman order?

BAKER. Which he should have disobeyed?

WALLACE. Defense motion is denied.

BAKER. (*With restrained, deliberate fury.*) Of course denied. It is now plain enough why the government has chosen to try Captain Wirz on a conspiracy charge. On that charge the accused may be convicted without any direct evidence against him ——

WALLACE. (*Rising.*) Mr. Baker!

BAKER. (*Going on.*) —and if there is a conspiracy, it is one directed against Capt. Wirz. I say now that the motives which bring Wirz to trial here dishonor the government of the United States; and that contradicting its own military code—the Army will have this man though he was only doing his proper duty.

WALLACE. Are you through, Mr. Baker?

BAKER. I am through, sir.

WALLACE. You have been in contempt since the beginning of that outburst. The Court will consider a formal charge against you.

34

You are dismissed from this proceeding forthwith, and will immediately leave this room.

BAKER. Let Captain Wirz be without counsel—so this trial may be judged for what it is ——

WALLACE. (*Not waiting for Baker to finish.*) Guards—escort Mr. Baker from the room. (*Sits. Baker starts for the door, his manner cool. He stops there on Chipman's speech.*)

WIRZ. I appeal the Court! I will have no counsel (*And then, almost with satisfaction.*) —no counsel then. It makes no difference. (*The Judges glance at one another. The dilemma is theirs.*)

CHIPMAN. (*Rises.*) I respectfully request the Court . . . (*Baker halts at the door.*) The Court has borne the provocative behavior of defense counsel with the utmost patience—I request that Mr. Baker be allowed to purge himself of contempt if he so wishes. (*Making his meaning clear despite the elaborate phrasing.*) I pray that the magnanimity of the Court extend itself so that not even in the wildest misrepresentation of this trial may it be said this defendant was denied counsel of his choice. (*Sits.*)

WALLACE. (*After a pause.*) Mr. Baker. For the single reason that Mr. Wirz may have counsel of his choice you may now purge yourself of contempt if you so wish. You may do so by recanting those remarks impugning the integrity of the government and army of the United States, by apologizing to the Court and by giving us your oath such outbursts will not occur again.

BAKER. (*With great deliberateness.*) I do so recant and apologize and give my oath that I will not hereafter impugn the fairness of the Court or the motives of the government and Army of the United States. (*He crosses to table, R., sits.*)

WALLACE. The Judge Advocate will —— (*Notices witness.*) Are we through with this witness? (*Both lawyers indicate that they are.*) The Court thanks the witness and he may step down. (*Spencer exits.*) Call your next witness, Colonel. (*During the following speech the lights dim to out. Davidson takes his position in the witness chair and all personnel make necessary adjustments to indicate the passage of time.*)

CHIPMAN. On the specification that the defendant did keep in barbarously close confinement soldiers numbering at times forty thousand men without adequate shelter from the rain and heat of summer and the cold of winter we call . . .

DIM OUT. END OF SCENE 1

ACT I

SCENE 2

Some time later. The weather continues hot. The Court is assembled and the Witness, James Davidson, is being examined by Chipman as the act begins. Chipman examines with a driving desperate quality and an air of dishevelment.

CHIPMAN. (L. *of witness.*) Now, Mr. Davidson, Captain Wirz *knew* the dogs tore and killed prisoners of war?

DAVIDSON. It was commonly known, yes, sir.

CHIPMAN. Knew it, and permitted it, and as far as you know, never took steps to put an end to that practice —— (*Paces above Generals. Baker starts to object.*) Withdrawn! Mr. Davidson, during the time you were a prisoner at Andersonville, did you ever see a man torn by dogs—I mean on an occasion when Wirz was present?

DAVIDSON. Yes, sir.

CHIPMAN. Tell us about it.

DAVIDSON. (*Slowly, too slowly for Chipman.*) Saw that after tunnelling out of the stockade with another prisoner. We got maybe fifteen miles from the camp when the dogs treed us. The guards ordered us down. And I saw those dogs tear my companion.

CHIPMAN. And Captain Wirz was there, wasn't he?

DAVIDSON. Capt. Wirz rode up a minute after that pack of dogs had treed us, yelling "Get those Yankee bastards"—beggin' your pardon.

CHIPMAN. And he was present while those dogs were tearing your companion?

DAVIDSON. While they were tearing him, yes, sir.

CHIPMAN. And what was Wirz doing while they tore him ——?

DAVIDSON. Damning that man to hell—beg—his eyes starting out of his head—like a fit was on him.

CHIPMAN. (*Crosses to L. of Generals.*) Can you recall another instance—an instance where ——

WALLACE. (*His irritation is obvious.*) Before we hear the answer we will ask the Judge Advocate if he expects, as he stated yesterday, to conclude his case today ——

36

CHIPMAN. We shall make every effort to conclude ——
WALLACE. (*They are fighting now.*) The Court does not wish to exclude pertinent testimony but we have heard a great number of former Andersonville prisoners testify ——
CHIPMAN. (*Crosses to* L. *of witness.*) I am now trying to establish Mr. Wirz' attitude when he was present on occasions where extreme cruelty was practised —— The Court will understand that we call only those witnesses we think necessary . . .
WALLACE. Of course ——
CHIPMAN. —and we cannot altogether control the time required for thorough examination of witnesses ——
WALLACE. Naturally. However, the Court does not consider it necessary to hear further evidence corroborating facts alleged many times over. Will the government conclude this afternoon?
CHIPMAN. We will conclude this afternoon, sir.
WALLACE. Continue, Colonel.
CHIPMAN. Mr. Davidson, the question is, did you know of any instance where an escaped prisoner was tracked down and actually *killed* by dogs? And again, I am referring to an instance when Wirz was present. (*Davidson does not answer.*) Did you hear my question, Mr. Davidson?
DAVIDSON. Yes, sir.
CHIPMAN. Well?
DAVIDSON. I don't like to talk about that place, Colonel.
CHIPMAN. (*Curtly.*) State the circumstances. (*Crosses to table,* L., *sits.*)
DAVIDSON. Was this time a man from my prison squad escaped. Tunneling through to the outside one night. But then we heard the rumor he'd been captured by the dogs.
CHIPMAN. You actually saw that man being brought back to the stockade ——
DAVIDSON. Yes, sir. First through the gate is Captain Wirz on that big gray he rode and then come two guards and this man between them . . . And they was holding him . . . and letting him go once he was inside that gate . . . He fell down . . . his legs was torn and his throat laid open. His flesh torn about the legs and his neck bloody.
CHIPMAN. And did he get up or did he lie there?
DAVIDSON. Made as if to get up and then lay back. Didn't move after that.
CHIPMAN. And where was Wirz during all this time?

37

DAVIDSON. Right there.

CHIPMAN. Right *where*?

DAVIDSON. Like I said, sir ——

CHIPMAN. We will hear it again, *please*, Mr. Davidson.

DAVIDSON. Like I said, he rode in and this man fell down. Captain Wirz rode around him looking down at him, reining in his horse which was skittering and rearing—that was a horse with a temper—then rode back through the gate.

CHIPMAN. That will be all. Thank you.

BAKER. (*His manner is gentle in conscious contrast to Chipman's.*) Mr. Davidson, we will not detain you long, sir. In that first instance you have described—when you made your escape attempt—you say Captain Wirz cursed, urging on those dogs, that were tearing your companion.

DAVIDSON. Yes, sir.

BAKER. Tell me, Mr. Davidson, at any time in your career as a soldier—did you ever yell—"Get those rebel bastards"?

DAVIDSON. I guess so.

BAKER. And what was it that Captain Wirz yelled ——?

DAVIDSON. Get—those—Yankee—but that was different.

BAKER. How different?

DAVIDSON. He meant for those dogs to tear that man, and I saw them do that.

BAKER. You were close enough to see that ——

DAVIDSON. Yes ——

BAKER. Well—*how* close, would you say?

DAVIDSON. Ten, fifteen feet away maybe. No more'n from here to there.

BAKER. And how was it, Mr. Davidson, those dogs did not tear you? (*Davidson stares at Baker in shocked puzzled silence.*) How do you account for that? (*Davidson shakes his head inarticulately.*) Can you think of any reason, Mr. Davidson? (*More silence.*)

DAVIDSON. I wouldn't know why, sir.

BAKER. Now, since you admit those ferocious dogs didn't attack *you*, shall I understand you were completely unhurt when you were brought back to the camp?

DAVIDSON. (*Slowly.*) No, sir.

BAKER. You were bruised some, as a result of rushing pell-mell through the swamps, weren't you?

DAVIDSON. Yes.

BAKER. Bloodied a bit, too?

DAVIDSON. Some. From all that running and stumbling against rocks ——

BAKER. Yes. And from bramble bushes and whipping branches and dead cypress limbs, some of them as pointed as knives?

DAVIDSON. Yes, sir.

BAKER. It would bruise and bloody any man, trying to beat a pursuit through a Georgia swamp, wouldn't it?

DAVIDSON. I guess so.

BAKER. So in that second instance you spoke of, when you saw a man brought back to the stockade—couldn't those marks on him that you say were caused by the dogs—couldn't they have been caused by his rushing headlong through the swamps, as yours were?

DAVIDSON. That man was torn by dogs ——

BAKER. Well, now you didn't *see* him being torn by dogs, did you, Mr. Davidson?

DAVIDSON. It was commonly known that the dogs ——

BAKER. Many things are commonly known, sir. (*Rises. Crosses to* R. *of witness.*) Could you identify the bruises on this man as being indisputably caused by dogs?

DAVIDSON. (*Feebly stubborn.*) He was bit by the dogs and he died ——

BAKER. (*Shrugging. Crosses above table* R.) Possibly. How long did you remain at that spot after this man—you don't happen to know his name, do you?

DAVIDSON. No, sir.

BAKER. How long did you remain there after that man fell down?

DAVIDSON. Three—five minutes.

BAKER. And did you have occasion to look that way later?

DAVIDSON. Some time later—yes.

BAKER. And was he still lying there?

DAVIDSON. No, sir—taken off to the dead house ——

BAKER. Or to the sick ward? (*Waiting.*) Mr. Davidson, you can't say this man died as a result of being mutilated by dogs and you can't identify this man, is that correct?

DAVIDSON. (*To Wallace.*) Sir, please. I got to go back home.

BAKER. And Captain Wirz riding around that man . . . without a word—that sounds mighty unfeeling. You wouldn't know

39

whether he notified the guard at the gate to have that man moved, would you?

DAVIDSON. I got to go home.

BAKER. Thank you, Mr. Davidson. That will be all. (Sits R.)

CHIPMAN. (Rises—crosses to witness. His temper is barely under control.) Mr. Davidson, didn't Wirz openly show his contempt and hatred for men torn and killed by dogs? (Wirz reacts to Davidson.)

DAVIDSON. (Wretchedly.) I don't know.

CHIPMAN. You don't know? With Wirz coldly sitting his horse —indifferent to that man brought back to die ——

DAVIDSON. I can't say for sure how he felt.

CHIPMAN. (Hardly waiting for the answer.) But those were the marks of teeth and claws that you identified on that man, weren't they?

DAVIDSON. I guess so ——

CHIPMAN. (Shouting.) You were quite sure of all that at one time. You also said that he died—that the flies set on his face and he didn't move to brush them off ——

DAVIDSON. I don't remember ——

CHIPMAN. (With rising anger.) And Capt. Wirz looking on— looking on—that dying man.

DAVIDSON. I—I ——

CHIPMAN. All I am asking you to repeat is what you already have sworn to under oath—that his attitude was monstrously cold and indifferent to those dying men!

DAVIDSON. (High.) Let me be, Colonel.

CHIPMAN. Mr. Davidson, I must warn you ——!

DAVIDSON. (At absolute pitch.) I got to forget that place ——!

CHIPMAN. (Shouting at him.) Or has it been suggested to you that you forget that place ——

WALLACE. Colonel Chipman! I think the witness is through. (Chipman crosses L., sits shaken.) Are you now ill, Mr. Davidson?

DAVIDSON. (Steps off podium.) Yes, sir. I got pains ——

WALLACE. (Gently—pointedly looking at Chipman.) You have told us about that incident as well as you can now recall it, is that correct?

DAVIDSON. Yes, sir.

WALLACE. How old are you, Mr. Davidson?

DAVIDSON. Nineteen, sir.

WALLACE. I believe you said you fought with the 2nd Vermont Cavalry.
DAVIDSON. (*He straightens.*) The 2nd Vermont Cavalry, sir. We turned their flank many times.
WALLACE. You may now go home and the Court wishes you Godspeed in recovering good health and in forgetting what you have endured in war and in prison.
DAVIDSON. (*Starts* L., *stops, looks uncertainly from Chipman to Baker.*) Yes, sir. Thank you, sir. Could be those dogs didn't tear me for the same reason Daniel was not tore in the lion's den. There was many died in that place. Many died. I hear those dogs baying at night. I hear voices cry out "help, help" and no one to help. Many died. Many, many died.
CHIPMAN. (*After a silence, terribly strained.*) I apologize to the witness.
DAVIDSON. Yes, sir. (*He exits.*)
WALLACE. (*With deliberateness.*) The weather continues hot and we have been at this trial longer than anticipated. I will ascribe tempers to the heat. Call your next witness, Colonel.
CHIPMAN. Joseph Achuff to the stand ——
WALLACE. Is Mr. Achuff called to testify on the specification that dogs attacked escaping prisoners?
CHIPMAN. Yes, sir.
WALLACE. The Court considers it unnecessary to hear further testimony on that specification; it has been amply testified to by previous witnesses.
CHIPMAN. (*Rises.*) If the Court please——
WALLACE. That is the judgment of the Court. Call your next witness, Colonel. (*Chipman strides to the prosecution table.*)
CHIPMAN. (*To Hosmer.*) Who next?
HOSMER. Hardy.
CHIPMAN. Baker will roast him and toss him back to me well done.
HOSMER. (*With meaning: they have talked of this before.*) He won't roast Gray ——
CHIPMAN. So Gray is here . . . I won't put him on —— (*To the Court.*) As our final witness on the specification that defendant caused the death of prisoners by direct order, we call Jasper Culver to the stand. (*Sits. Wirz reacts.*)
LIEUTENANT. (*Calling out.*) Jasper Culver! (*Culver enters and is sworn in. There is a punchdrunk suggestion to the way he*

41

walks. *He smiles uncertainly. As Culver gets into his story, he will begin to act it out.)*

CHIPMAN. *(Seated.)* Mr. Culver, what was your regiment and when were you captured and brought to Andersonville?

CULVER. I was connected with the 67th N. Y. Infantry—and was captured and brought to Andersonville in March, 1864.

CHIPMAN. Did you ever see a prisoner of war killed? Inside the stockade?

CULVER. I did.

CHIPMAN. Who killed him?

CULVER. The guard.

CHIPMAN. And did that guard do so on his own or because of a direct order?

CULVER. He was given a direct order to kill him.

CHIPMAN. By whom?

CULVER. By Captain Wirz.

CHIPMAN. And where did that killing take place?

CULVER. At the deadline.

CHIPMAN. Who was the man you saw killed?

CULVER. We called him Chickamauga. Because he had lost a leg in that battle and because he had lost his memory there. So we called him by that name—Chickamauga.

CHIPMAN. And why did Chickamauga want to cross that line?

CULVER. He wished to lie down under a pine tree, he said, because a long time ago—but not that he could remember where—he had laid down under a pine tree. "I can't remember nothing before Chickamauga" is what he said to the guard . . .

CHIPMAN. State the circumstances—when did this occur?

CULVER. It was in the early fall, I believe . . . I remember the smell of burning leaves.

CHIPMAN. Continue, sir.

CULVER. I watched Chickamauga go toward the deadline and called to him to stop, but he went on as if not hearing. At the line he shouted to the sentry to let him cross, but the sentry waved him back. Chickamauga then began to move up and down the line, hopping back and forth on his one leg, begging to be let out of the stockade for ten minutes. The guard let him stay on the line but he was nervous and telling Chickamauga to get— *(He laughs.)* —back and Chickamauga laughed. And then Chickamauga, he said for the guard to tell Captain Wirz that he knew of a plot whereby all the men would escape and he would tell Captain Wirz about that plot in exchange for being let out a few minutes, and with that the guard called for the Captain to come. And Wirz came. And when Chickamauga saw Wirz he made the Captain promise to let him rest a few minutes under that pine tree if he tells him that plot and the Captain says he will do that, and then Chickamauga he says to the Captain, "I will tell you that plot to escape. Here it is in a nutshell. Why, you know Uncle Billy Sherman in his white socks is marching through Georgia and what he is going to do is blast Andersonville open from the outside and that is how the men will get free." And Wirz began to rave and he said to Chickamauga, "I am going to give you a pass to hell" and Chickamauga said, "You can't give me no pass to hell on account I'm in hell now." And Captain Wirz turned to the guard and said, "Get that man back across the line or shoot him." The guard said, "I can't shoot no cripple." And Captain Wirz said, "If you don't obey I will have you court-martialed." And the next thing the guard shot Chickamauga and he fell over the deadline. Done for.

CHIPMAN. That will be all.

BAKER. Mr. Culver, I am thinking of how accurately you told that story. You remember the details down to the exact words said back and forth. That sense of detail makes you a most excellent witness.

CULVER. Thank you, sir.

BAKER. And one might add—it is also the characteristic of a good soldier—which I am sure you were before Andersonville ——

CULVER. (*Echoing in mingled emotions of pain and pride.*) Before Andersonville!

BAKER. When you were in the line.

CULVER. (*Beginning to chant.*) In the line! Antietam Bridge, Chancellorsville and Stafford Court House ——

BAKER. And you must remember the nighttime bivouacs, around the fires, listening to the sentries ——

CULVER. Around the fires! Hearing them calling through the dark, "All is well"—post one to post two, "All is well"——

BAKER. And that outpost line—that of course was a line which a man dare not cross on pain of being shot by the sentries ——

CULVER. On pain of being shot by the sentries!—— And "who goes there" is the cry, "Who goes there?" "Who goes ——"

BAKER. And of course you can tell us why such lines are set up

43

by commanding officers, Mr. Culver. As you remember it, sir, by the book.

CULVER. (*Very correct, sounding out.*) By the book, sir —— And that is for the order and safety of the camp.

BAKER. And inside the stockade at Andersonville—were there signs posted warning men not to cross the line?

CULVER. (*With an air of modesty.*) I recall some—yes, Counsel, there were.

BAKER. That story you told about Chickamauga. With the great interest people have in anecdotes about the war, you have undoubtedly had occasion to tell it a number of times already, Mr. Culver, haven't you?

CULVER. I have been requested to tell it a number of times.

BAKER. I'll wager you could tell it a hundred times and it would come out exactly as you told it today ——

CULVER. A thousand times, Counsel, and it would come out the same way.

BAKER. And always told with great effect, I imagine.

CULVER. With great effect, yes, sir.

BAKER. It would hardly be as effective if Captain Wirz did not come out the villain of the piece, would it?

CULVER. Hardly —— (*Starting—staring at Baker—and a grim sober expression coming into his face.*) You wish to make a fool of me, Counsel. I'm not lying ——

BAKER. (*In a sad anger.*) No, Mr. Culver, you are not. A man can't help it if fables grow in his head, can he?

CULVER. No, he—*fables?*—I don't know what you're talking about ——!

BAKER. (*Moving to address the Court.*) I'm looking for facts and I'm hunting for them through fairy tales of good and evil —— Mr. Culver, you say you heard Captain Wirz say, "Get that man back across the line or shoot him." Didn't Wirz actually say "*For God's sakes,* get that man back across the line or you will have to shoot him"?

CULVER. It is frozen into my memory as I have said it ——

BAKER. And when Chickamauga said, "I am in hell now," didn't Wirz say, "You and I both"—"you and I both are in hell"—as indeed they both were?

CULVER. I have said it as I remember it ——!

BAKER. As you need to remember it. That will be all, Mr.

44

Culver, thank you. Move to dismiss all counts under this specification since the deadline was a proper military line required for the order and safety of that camp.

CHIPMAN. (Rises—front of Generals.) It was not a purely military line! Mr. Culver, look at the map. Where the stream entered the camp under the west wall. There! What was that water like?

CULVER. (Dazed.) Somewhat fast-flowing, yes, sir.

CHIPMAN. Was it drinkable?

CULVER. Somewhat drinkable, yes, sir. (Points to Baker.) That man there!——

CHIPMAN. And inside the deadline, what was the water like there?

CULVER. Not fittin' to drink, no sir.

CHIPMAN. It was by that time filthy and clogged with waste matter—driving the men to do what—?

CULVER. To try for a drink near the west wall.

CHIPMAN. (Crosses above witness to R.) And they had to wade waist-deep through that swamp to get that drink of water, didn't they?

CULVER. Waist-deep and further ——

CHIPMAN. And when they succeeded in getting to that water, what did the guards do?

CULVER. Opened fire on us—yes ——

CHIPMAN. Killing men?

CULVER. Killing and wounding—yes, yes!

CHIPMAN. Killing and wounding for a drink of water! And Wirz knew that and he let those men get shot down, didn't he?—And Counsel calls that a purely military line! (Crosses to table L.) Move to deny defense motion as to that deadline in that it was clearly part of the cold, inhuman design of that camp.

BAKER. (Rises.) Inhuman?

CHIPMAN. Yes.

BAKER. Immoral?

CHIPMAN. Yes.

WIRZ. I can explain ——

BAKER. (Gesturing to quiet Wirz. To Chipman.) Will the Judge Advocate openly and finally admit his belief that Captain Wirz' duty was to make a moral, not a military choice?

CHIPMAN. The human choice.

WALLACE. This arguing over an irrelevant issue becomes intolerable—parties are warned. Defense motion denied. (*Baker crosses* R., *sits.*) The Judge Advocate will now state the connection between the moral issue and the charge of conspiracy.
CHIPMAN. (*Sits. After a pause; tired.*) The Judge Advocate will not attempt to make that connection.
WALLACE. Thank you, Mr. Culver, you may stand down. (*Culver exits.*) If you have concluded your case, Colonel, we will now adjourn until tomorrow morning, at which time the defense will be ready ——
CHIPMAN. We may wish to call further witnesses ——
WALLACE. If so they will be witnesses bringing in new criminal evidence. I say *new* criminal evidence in the precise legal meaning of the term, bearing *directly* on the charge of conspiracy. I hope that is understood.
CHIPMAN. Yes, sir.
WALLACE. The Court stands adjourned. (*General exits. Counsel remains in the room. Baker takes hat from rack,* U. R. *and crosses* D.)
BAKER. The choices in this world are bitter, Colonel, aren't they? On the one hand to follow your decent instincts and on the other —— (R. *of witness chair.*) Tell me, if you can, Colonel, how does your role in this room differ from Wirz' at Andersonville—seeing that he too did nothing more nor less than carry out policy?
CHIPMAN. You compare me to him?
BAKER. You know in your heart that you condemn him only for carrying out the orders of his superior. (*Crosses below chair to Chipman.*) You have as much as said so. But this Court will have no part of that argument. And what then do you do but withdraw it? You obey, as Wirz obeyed.
CHIPMAN. You compare me to him?
BAKER. Oh, of course, you're governed by purer motives. After all, you're on the edge of a brilliant career. You'll walk out of this case the envy of every struggling young lawyer in the country; the successful prosecutor of the one war criminal to be hanged out of this war. Yes, your future's assured . . . if you don't jeopardize it. Shall the government's own counsel at this time preach disobedience to orders? How does it feel to be an instrument of policy, nothing more?

CHIPMAN. Goddamn you ——
BAKER. Get as angry as you wish—that's the truth of it. Good afternoon, gentlemen. (*Baker and Schade exit. Chipman crosses to Judges' table.*)
HOSMER. Don't you see what he's trying to do? Provoke you into playing the idealist here?
CHIPMAN. (*Moves* R.) I see ——
HOSMER. It would suit him perfectly to lead you down that path ——
CHIPMAN. (*Moves* R.) I know ——
HOSMER. —to turn things so it's you arguing with the government ——
CHIPMAN. All right! (*Chipman moves to* L. *Starts to close doors, brings himself under control.*) I shout at you—I shout at Davidson—only a boy—a sick boy . . . (*He is silent for a long moment. Crosses to table,* L., *sits.*) Where do we stand after days of those witnesses we've put on—those sick, broken survivors of that place? We haven't really proved conspiracy and we haven't proved criminal acts. And yet I know that behind Wirz's screams of innocence and persecution—behind that stance of the honorable wounded soldier who was only obeying orders, he hides something dark that must be smoked out—I ask you: What kind of a case do we bring in here?
HOSMER. If you want a better one, close with Gray. (*As Chipman looks knowingly at him.*) Eyewitness evidence that Wirz murdered ——
CHIPMAN. (*Withering.*) Eyewitness evidence ——
HOSMER. Let the Court decide ——
CHIPMAN. You've heard Gray—do you believe him?
HOSMER. Let the Court decide ——! (*Hosmer watches Chipman move restlessly.*) If you put him on you will finish strong. Gray furnishes the name of the murdered man; name and regiment. Good God, what difference does it make in the end, Chipman? Wirz is doomed anyway.
CHIPMAN. And the kind of case we bring doesn't matter, does it?
HOSMER. Not—really.
CHIPMAN. (*Flaring.*) But if there's a moral issue here—I mean if we feel that Wirz should have disobeyed—and if we evade that issue—if we're afraid to raise it—how are we actually any better

47

than that creature was at Andersonville? Are we all Wirz under the skin? Feeding where we're kept alive? At a trough?

HOSMER. So Baker *has* reached you!

CHIPMAN. (*With hard amusement.*) Do you think that? Or is it that he raises an issue which has been in this case from the beginning—and which we haven't wanted to face?

HOSMER. We don't *need* to face it. I'll say it again—Wirz is doomed no matter how our case looks. But you can make it hard for yourself if you turn it the wrong way. You're a soldier, you know how the Army has to function, if it is to function at all. It has ways of dealing with irregulars. Are you thinking of a Washington career or will you be satisfied with a law practice in some county seat in Iowa? (*Studying Chipman.*) Chipman, you seem to *want* to go a hard way.

CHIPMAN. (*Moves to front of witness chair.*) *I want to go a hard way.* This blood-spattered country—bleaching skulls in the woods —the dead of my own Iowa 2nd, names you wouldn't know—did any of us *want* to go a hard way? (*Moves* L.) But we did—we did! As if we had any choice . . . as if I have any choice here. I asked for this case feeling *hard* against them—hating them enough to want to flog them through Wirz. Do you think I *want* to shed that hatred? Understanding what Baker wants to do—to lock me in a quarrel with the government—I still can't go around that issue. (*Moves* R. *to couch.*) I hate that damned Southern cause— and still I can't go around what Baker says. I'm partisan to my bones—and still *I can't go around it.* I'd like to believe I'm more of a man than Wirz was; that, had I been in his place, I would have disobeyed if that was all that was left me to do to save those men . . . Yes, that's what sticks me. Am I more of a man than he was? (*Crosses to table,* L.) Either . . . either I press the Court to consider the issue of Wirz' moral responsibility to disobey or— I'm no better in my mind than he was! I can't go around *that.*

HOSMER. And just how do you plan to go around raising the moral issue?

CHIPMAN. (*Crosses to couch,* R.) I don't know —— (*Reaching for something.*) Let Baker put Wirz on the stand.

HOSMER. Which he won't do . . .

CHIPMAN. (*Crosses to* R.) I know that. I know . . .

HOSMER. Put on Gray. You don't have to like him . . . Just put him on. Nail down your case with a clear statement of

murder—and you will have your man . . . even if it's not in YOUR way —— The government has a point to make too you know—it struggles to pull together a divided country. Isn't that a worthy, an important thing? At least as important as the purity of your soul? (*Goes to door.*) Do you stay?
CHIPMAN. A moment . . . There are larger issues than a man's own convictions. Aren't there?
HOSMER. (*Tiredly.*) Sometimes. (*A pause, and then, almost fiercely.*) You make me feel old. (*He exits. Chipman walks slowly to witness chair, sits in it, looks at Andersonville map, then at Wirz' couch, raises his arms in a small gesture of frustration and doubt, and then lowers them onto the arms of the chair as the*)

CURTAIN FALLS—END OF ACT ONE

ACT II

SCENE 1

SCENE: *The following morning.*

AT RISE: *The court personnel, lawyers and reporters stand about, chatting, waiting for the session to begin. The Lieutenant enters.*

LIENTENANT. Attention! (*The Judges enter.*)
WALLACE. At ease. (*Judges, et al. take their positions.*) This Court is now in session. What is the pleasure of the Judge Advocate?
CHIPMAN. (*Standing.*) If it please the Court . . . on the specification that the defendant committed murder by his own hand, we call Sergeant James S. Gray.
LIEUTENANT. (*Calling out into corridor.*) Sergeant James S. Gray. (*During the following exchange, Gray enters and waits by door until told to be sworn it.*)
BAKER. (*Seated.*) If the Court please, we do not see that name listed here.
CHIPMAN. (*Moving to General's table, his voice noncommittal.*) Sergeant Gray was not listed since it was uncertain that his release from duty could be arranged in time. He is attached to General Thomas' headquarters at Nashville. (*Wallace glances inquiringly at Baker.*)
BAKER. No objection.
WALLACE. The witness may be sworn in. (*Gray enters, salutes the Court smartly, is sworn and takes the stand.*)
CHIPMAN. (*Standing table L. The tone is flat.*) Sergeant Gray, what is your regiment?
GRAY. Seventh Illinois Cavalry, Company B, sir.
CHIPMAN. And how long have you been in the service?
GRAY. In my last term, two years and one month.

50

CHIPMAN. How long were you at Andersonville prison, Sergeant?

GRAY. I was taken to Andersonville on the 10th of June, 1864, and remained there until November.

CHIPMAN. Do you know anything about the defendant, Wirz, having shot a prisoner of war there at any time? (*Wirz tries to rise, Baker restrains him.*)

GRAY. (*His manner is calm and easy.*) He shot a young fellow named William Stewart, a private belonging to the Ninth Minnesota Infantry.

CHIPMAN. State the circumstances.

GRAY. Stewart and I went out of the stockade with a dead body ——

CHIPMAN. Explain how you could get out.

GRAY. The regulations were that whenever a man died, prisoners could be detailed to take the body out past the gate to the deadhouse.

CHIPMAN. Continue, sir.

GRAY. Well, sir, I had begged for the chance to move that dead body and I was picked with Stewart to take it out. We went up to the gate with the dead man and they passed us out with a guard. It was my determination—I don't know whether it was Stewart's or not—to try to make an escape again. We went toward the deadhouse, not to put the body into the deadhouse because in that house they were piled like cordwood full up and the line of dead bodies extended out from it about fifty yards. Wirz then came riding up and dismounted and asked us what we were doing out there. Stewart replied that we had brought out a dead body to place in the deadhouse. Wirz said it was a lie, that we were trying to make our escape. Stewart said it was not so. We came for purpose stated. Wirz said if you say that again I'll blow your brains out. Stewart repeated what he said before. Wirz then struck him down and stamped him and then drew his revolver and shot him ——

CHIPMAN. (*Pointing to Wirz.*) Is that the man?

GRAY. Yes. (*Wirz, in a spasm of energy, leans forward facing Gray.*)

WIRZ. Look close, Sergeant—make sure! I give you the chance to take back that lie before the great God judges you!

GRAY. (*Cool and indifferent.*) You knocked him down and shot him dead ——

CHIPMAN. That will be all. (*Sits L. Baker addresses the Court.*)

BAKER. (*Rises.*) I ask for a moment to confer with the defendant. We have no preparation for this witness. (*Wallace signals affirmatively.*) Quick, who is Gray?

WIRZ. It's no use ——

BAKER. Who is Gray?

WIRZ. I don't know.

BAKER. What about Stewart?

WIRZ. There was no William Stewart.

BAKER. Are you sure?

WIRZ. Yes—yes. I'm sure.

BAKER. (*Turning toward Gray. Restlessly searching.*) Sergeant, will you describe once more this so-called Stewart's death?

GRAY. Captain Wirz rode up and asked us by what authority we were out there. Stewart spoke up and said we were out there by proper authority ——

BAKER. (*His manner sharper, openly skeptical.*) So Captain Wirz knocked him down and shot him simply because he said he was out there by proper authority?

GRAY. Whether he shot Stewart because he said that to him or because he was a Yankee, I don't know. I don't know why Wirz shot him. I leave that to himself. But that was all Stewart said to him.

BAKER. (*Rises—crosses to Gray.*) There were some guards about when this so-called murder occurred, were there not?

GRAY. I recall some.

BAKER. Did you speak to them after Stewart was killed?

GRAY. I never spoke to Johnny Reb if I didn't have to.

BAKER. How well did you know Stewart?

GRAY. (*Shrugging.*) We were in the same prison squad.

BAKER. (*Crosses to L. of witness.*) And under what circumstance did he oblige you with his name and regiment?

GRAY. I don't recollect exactly.

BAKER. (*Crosses front of Gray to his L.*) Describe this William Stewart.

GRAY. All looked alike there. Thinned out and not to be recognized by their own mothers ——

BAKER. (*Crosses above Gray to his R.*) So you cannot describe him. You talked to him and you know his name and regiment but you cannot describe this man. Did he hide his face while he talked to you? (*Crosses to Gray's* L. *As Gray wants to speak.*) I know—thinned out and not to be recognized by their own mothers. Can you refer to any third person who could identify this William Stewart?

GRAY. No.

BAKER. No! What does that answer mean? There were ninety men in that prison squad with you and Stewart. (*Crosses to Gray's* R.) Then other men—at least one—must have known he was from the Ninth Minnesota—and could identify him.

GRAY. Counsel, he happened to mention his name and regiment to me ——

BAKER. (*Crosses to Gray's* L. *Through his teeth.*) However, fortunately for the prosecution which until now has lacked for a clear criminal instance, it has dredged you up as the single witness to the murder of a man having at least a name —— (*Very hard.*) Sergeant, do you believe in an after-life and that man's sins, including the sin of lying, will there be punished?

GRAY. I believe there is such a thing as punishment after death ——

BAKER. Have you ever been arrested for a criminal offense?

GRAY. No, sir.

BAKER. I gather you like Army life, seeing that you have re-enlisted.

GRAY. I would say that.

BAKER. (*Crosses to witness'* R.) After all, the Army feeds you, keeps you comfortable, and judging by your sergeant's stripes, you are considered by your superiors to be a good soldier, one who knows what he is supposed to do without it being explained to him in so many words.

GRAY. A man gets to know what is expected of him.

BAKER. And if you felt—even if you weren't told—what was expected of you, you would carry it out, wouldn't you?

GRAY. Certainly.

BAKER. And if you felt—even if you weren't told—what the Army's real concern was in some situation and if you understood that to mean that you were supposed to lie ——

WALLACE. Finish your question along that line, Mr. Baker, and you will be in contempt ——

BAKER. Withdrawn. Sergeant, what did you do before entering the Army?

GRAY. Farmed some; ran dogs.

BAKER. Ran dogs ——?

GRAY. In hunting and so forth.

BAKER. Where did you do that work?

GRAY. In Illinois, Indiana, Virginia, and ——

BAKER. Virginia . . . Virginia —— (*Crosses to table* R.) For what purpose did you run your dogpack in Virginia? Was it by any chance to bring back runaway slaves?

GRAY. Yes, sir.

BAKER. I take it it was more profitable to track down runaway slaves in Virginia than to hunt deer in Indiana.

GRAY. Yes, sir. Being as the nigra was valuable property that had to be brought back alive.

BAKER. Tell me, Sergeant. Did that valuable property ever make human sounds when you caught it and beg you to let it find freedom?

GRAY. I don't remember.

BAKER. Human feelings must be put aside sometimes, mustn't they? (*Gray doesn't answer.*) And the truth must be put aside sometimes, too. (*Gray doesn't answer.*) And when you said you saw Wirz kill a man named Stewart at Andersonville, you were lying, weren't you?

GRAY. I saw that happen as I have described it.

BAKER. That will be all.

CHIPMAN. (*Rises—crosses to witness.*) Sergeant Gray! *Were* you lying when you said you saw Wirz kill a man named Stewart?

GRAY. I saw that happen as I have described it.

CHIPMAN. Sergeant, did you see Wirz kill a man named Stewart or did you hear about something like that?

GRAY. I saw that happen as I described it—*Sir!*

CHIPMAN. . . . That will be all.

WALLACE. (*With distaste.*) The witness will step down. (*Gray rises, salutes the Court and exits.*) Has the Judge Advocate finally concluded his case?

CHIPMAN. (*Crosses to table,* R.—*sits.*) Yes, sir.

WALLACE. Is the defense ready?

BAKER. Yes, sir. (*Rises—crosses to above witness chair.*) If the court please, since defense regards the instance of murder alleged against the defendant as the single charge worth refuting ——

WALLACE. The Court is not interested in your judgment of the charges ——
BAKER. (*Finishing*.) —we shall waive our entire list of witnesses and will in their place put on the stand one witness.
WALLACE. One witness? (*Wirz stirs restlessly and turns to Baker as if to speak.*)
BAKER. Questioning will take no more than a few minutes and will constitute the entire defense case.
WALLACE. Who is the witness?
BAKER. He is in the room—Dr. Ford, the physician in charge at the Old Capitol jail, where the defendant has been lodged since the trial began. (*Protest from Wirz to Baker, who quiets him. Chipman and Hosmer exchange puzzled glances.*)
WALLACE. Let Dr. Ford take the stand. (*Ford steps forward and is sworn.*)
BAKER. (*Seated.*) Dr. Ford, have you, during some time past, been in the habit of seeing the defendant?
FORD. Since June, I believe, ever since his imprisonment he has been under my care when sick.
BAKER. Have you during that time examined his right arm and have you examined him today?
FORD. Yes, sir.
BAKER. What do you find to be the condition of his right arm?
FORD. It is swollen and inflamed; ulcerated in three places; and it has the appearance of having been broken.
BAKER. The fingers of his right hand?
FORD. Two fingers, the little finger and the next are slightly contracted. The contraction is due to injury of the nerve leading down to the fingers.
BAKER. Have you examined the defendant's left shoulder?
FORD. Yes, sir. A portion of it is dead. There is a very large scar on the left shoulder and a portion of deltoid muscle is entirely gone—I suppose from his war wound. It has been carried away, only the front part of the muscle remaining.
BAKER. How does that influence the strength of the arm?
FORD. (*Illustrating.*) He might be able to strike out with forearm from the elbow but he could not elevate the whole arm.
BAKER. And as to the right arm? Would he be capable with that arm of pushing or knocking a man down?
FORD. I should think him incapable of doing so with either arm, without doing himself great injury.

BAKER. Would he have been capable of using with force any heavy or light instrument—would he have been capable of pulling the trigger—let alone suffering the recoil of—a heavy revolver?

FORD. No—not likely.

BAKER. And as to his condition a year ago, in 1864?

FORD. I have spoken with Dr. Bates, who was at Andersonville and who examined Wirz there at the defendant's request, and he confirms my opinion that this condition was no better in 1864 than it is now.

BAKER. (*Rises.*) Then he could not have knocked down this so-called William Stewart ——

FORD. I don't see how ——

BAKER. He could not have pulled the trigger ——

FORD. As I have said ——

BAKER. He could not have killed him. The defense rests! Thank you! (*Sits.*)

WALLACE. (*Harsh and strained.*) Will the judge advocate cross-examine?

CHIPMAN. (*Seated.*) Dr. Ford has testified to Mr. Wirz's physical condition as he saw it and we are not here to dispute medical findings. No cross-examination, but . . . (*His voice dies away.*)

WALLACE. (*Waits, and then—*) Thank you, Dr. Ford. (*Ford returns to his seat,* U R.)

WIRZ. (*To Baker, a loud whisper.*) What is it? Is it all finished? But I have not had the chance ——

WALLACE. We will convene the day after tomorrow to hear government and defense summations.

CHIPMAN. (*In a burst.*) If the Court please, we ask for a continuance ——!

WALLACE. Continuance?

CHIPMAN. —until tomorrow morning. The Judge Advocate would like to determine if there is something pertinent to this trial ——

WALLACE. Does the judge advocate wish to bring forward new evidence?

CHIPMAN. Possibly.

BAKER. The defense will welcome new evidence—particularly on the charge of violent murder attributed to a man who cannot raise his arms.

WALLACE. (*Gavel.*) Unless the government contemplates other

56

witnesses we must consider the presentation of evidence is finished —— (*Wirz reacts.*)

CHIPMAN. (*Glancing rapidly at Wirz, his manner terribly strained, speaking in bursts of thought.*) We do not feel that the situation at Andersonville has been thoroughly explored—that is why we ask the continuance—we feel there is more to be discovered—more to be said about what took place there ——

WIRZ. I agree—yes! For once I agree with the Judge Advocate! (*Wallace raps.*)

CHIPMAN. (*Crosses to L. of couch.*) Does the defendant desire to take the stand in his own behalf?

WIRZ. What?

BAKER. What is that? . . . No, the defendant will not take the stand.

CHIPMAN. (*Looking straight at Wirz, speaking with desperate speed.*) Of course he is not legally bound to do so, but it seems to the Judge Advocate that he might wish to make his position clearer than anyone else can possibly do for him ——

BAKER. (*Rises.*) What is the Judge Advocate trying to do ——?

WIRZ. (*Leans toward Chipman.*) If I might wish what? What——?

(Over-lap.)
> BAKER. (*Going on.*) He addresses defendant over the head of counsel.
> WIRZ. (*Overlap on above cue "counsel."*) But what is it the Judge Advocate is saying —— I would like to know what is meant—that I might make my position clearer ——?

WALLACE. (*The gavel rapping.*) You cannot speak unless you take the stand, Mr. Wirz. The Judge Advocate is asking if you wish to take the stand. You have a right to do so, but cannot be compelled to do so. You have that right, though we suggest you listen to counsel. (*Baker crosses to R. of Wirz, sits on couch. Chipman turns back to table, L.*)

BAKER. Are you out of your mind?

SCHADE. (*Crosses to L. of couch.*) I don't understand what's come over you!

WIRZ. This legal game has been played back and forth and I am to die without a word to say for myself! I must explain ——

BAKER. Listen. The evidence they've offered is tainted from start to finish. And they know it! Let them bring in their verdict of guilty. But it must then go to the President, who may pardon as he values the reputation of the government. That's your single chance ——

WIRZ. And I say no chance. No chance ——

SCHADE. Wirz, listen to Baker ——

BAKER. You will not take the stand ——

WIRZ. (*Rises.*) I was a man like other men and I wish to show that!

BAKER. (*Rises.*) You'll face Chipman alone. You will be alone ——

SCHADE. (*Overlaps.*) Do you understand? Alone!!

WIRZ. Yes, alone, as I have been alone—and neither you nor anyone here has been concerned for me as a *man.* And now —— (*His manner is feverish. To Court.*) I might wish to speak— (*Crosses to* R. *of witness chair.*) —since the Judge Advocate wishes me to take the stand ——

WALLACE. I don't understand you, Mr. Wirz. You may or may not take the stand as *you* wish. It has nothing to do with what the Judge Advocate wishes.

WIRZ. And I am saying that I might do that. Since I have been slandered here I might do that. I don't understand what is the difficulty —— (*Revealing his need, in spite of a tone of mockery. Crosses to Judges' table.*) So the Judge Advocate wants me to take the stand ——

WALLACE. The Judge Advocate can not influence you to do that. He is not your counsel.

WIRZ. No, no, of course he is not. He is my worst enemy. Oh, I know that. He wishes to destroy me. (*He looks steadily at Chipman and Chipman in turn looks back at him. There is something private between them now.*) Take the stand, on my own behalf, eh, Colonel?

CHIPMAN. On your own behalf.

BAKER. (*Crosses to* L. *of couch, grimly.*) Are you dispensing with counsel, Capt. Wirz?

CHIPMAN. (*Speaking with cool desperate calculation.*) Mr. Wirz, if you take the stand, you will speak for yourself. And after that— let me warn you—I will try to search you out to the bottom of your soul.

WIRZ. Hah! You think you can do that?

CHIPMAN. I can try ——

WALLACE. (*Gavel.*) Will the defendant say whether or not he wishes to take the stand!

WIRZ. General! (*Crosses to Baker—L. of couch.*) Hah—do you hear that? My worst enemy—what does he say? He will search me out, to the bottom of my soul!

BAKER. You think Chipman is here to save you?

WIRZ. I am to die—I must take the stand! I have been made a monster in the eyes of my children. I die with that mark on me if I do not speak up! And I will not have it that way —— I will give them my words so they can say their father was a man like other men. Do you understand me? (*Baker looks at Wirz searchingly. Wirz's tone is strange.*) You will examine—and then I will fight him.

BAKER. And if you take the stand . . . how will I keep you from saying more than you should?

WIRZ. But you see, Baker, I must fight him . . . (*Baker stares hard at Wirz.*) I must . . . fight him. (*Baker shrugs finally, his expression tired and a little sad. He turns to face the Court.*)

BAKER. (*To Wallace, slowly.*) The defendant will take the stand in his own behalf.

WALLACE. He understands that he is not required to do so?

BAKER. The defendant understands and wishes to do so.

WALLACE. You may take the stand, Mr. Wirz. (*Wirz is sworn and takes the stand.*)

BAKER. (*His style is curt. His effort is to be brief and to not allow Wirz to say too much.*) Capt. Wirz, you are a naturalized citizen of the United States, is that correct?

WIRZ. Yes, sir.

BAKER. When and where were you born?

WIRZ. I was born in Zurich, Switzerland, in the year 1822.

BAKER. What year did you arrive in the United States?

WIRZ. In 1849.

BAKER. Describe briefly your activities prior to the outbreak of the war.

WIRZ. I worked at first in the mills in Lawrence, Massachusetts, and, not doing well there, moved with my family to various parts of the United States. I lived in Louisiana for a time and resided in Louisville, Kentucky, when the war broke out.

BAKER. State your war record prior to your appointment as superintendent of the Andersonville prison camp.

WIRZ. I enlisted in the service of the Confederacy as a private and was soon commissioned as a lieutenant, having had previous military training abroad. After being wounded at the battle of Seven Pines I was offered that assignment of superintendent, by General Winder.

BAKER. Over what period of time did you serve in that assignment?

WIRZ. From January, 1864, until February, 1865.

BAKER. Were you at any time given special or secret instructions as to how you were to run that camp?

WIRZ. No sir!

BAKER. I refer specifically to instructions for the care of the prisoners.

WIRZ. No, sir—no special instructions beyond the prescribed regulations for the care of prisoners of war, and any statement to the contrary ——

BAKER. (Breaking in.) Captain Wirz, were the food supplies at first furnished you sufficient for the prisoners?

WIRZ. Yes, sir, at first I was given ample supplies to furnish for each and every enemy prisoner a ration which was the same ration issued to Confederate soldiers as is the custom. It included bacon and fresh baked bread daily. If not bacon, it was beef and those men did not starve, but later it became ——

BAKER. Capt. Wirz, state the circumstances under which that situation changed.

WIRZ. It began to change for the worse around March when we began to receive prisoners by the thousands but not sufficiently an increase in the ration. So I naturally had to cut down more and more that ration and I wrote to General Winder about that ——

BAKER. When did you write that letter?

WIRZ. Some time in May, 1864.

BAKER. (Holding up letter.) I have here a letter written by Capt. Wirz to Gen. Winder, dated May 26, 1864. (Schade takes letter to Wallace.)

SCHADE. Presented to the court.

WALLACE. (After glancing at it.) It may be entered in the record.

SCHADE. (Giving letter to court clerk.) Letter of May 26, 1864, offered for the defense.

CLERK. Exhibit nine, for the defense.

BAKER. Capt. Wirz, tell us about that letter.

WIRZ. Yes, sir. I wrote to General Winder about the lack of food and requested additional supplies.

BAKER. Now, Captain, did General Winder reply to that letter?

WIRZ. He did so in person on one of his visits to the camp. He said we were taking care of the prisoners just as well as the enemy took care of *our* men in *their* hands. He said he had reports that our men were not well-treated, particularly at a camp at Elmira, New York, where they were dying like flies. He was in a temper and he made it clear *that* closed the subject, and as an inferior officer I felt I could not pursue the matter further. However, I did what was in my power to do there—as about those drummer boys ——

BAKER. We will get to that in a moment. Tell the Court now the origin of the deadline.

WIRZ. Yes, as to that deadline. Well—in that conversation I said to Gen. Winder that the prisoners were getting desperate because of the lack of food and the guards consequently nervous, fearing a rush on the walls, and there was bound to be trouble. I asked for more guards there to quiet the prisoners down with a show of strength. But he said men could not be spared. But still—it was my responsibility they should not escape, don't you see, so I suggested that inner line, and General Winder approved that line. But that did not mean I did not consider those prisoners, as I started to say before about those drummer boys ——

BAKER. (*Curtly.*) Very well. Tell the Court about those drummer boys.

WIRZ. Yes, sir. There were sixty or seventy boys in that camp, drummer boys, little bits of boys and I felt bad that these boys, no more than children, should suffer there, having children of my own. So I asked them if they would take an oath not to try to escape and they did and they were put on parole outside the walls and lived outside the camp. I assigned them to pick black-berries to provide additional food for the camp, but that did not work. Being boys they ate what they picked themselves —— And that was not all I did there ——

BAKER. (*Trying to control Wirz.*) Capt. Wirz. Tell us about Father Whelan ——

WIRZ. Yes. I gave permission for all priests and ministers to enter that camp and Father Whelan, of the Roman Catholic Church, came several times bringing fresh bread there. He was allowed to bring that in and he distributed it to all the prisoners, black and white. All religious people of any denomination were permitted to enter to give comfort to the prisoners—all. I believe that religion is—that religion ——

BAKER. Now, Captain, tell us about the women who tried to bring food into the camp.

WIRZ. Yes, yes —— General Winder at first graciously consented to let that food in, but when those women were about to do that he received some bad war news, some report that Sheridan was burning farmhouses and crops in the Shenandoah Valley and he then flew into a rage and said that food couldn't be brought in and being an inferior there I could hardly override his orders. That is how it was. In general that place was entirely on my head ——

BAKER. Did you try to get relieved ——?

WIRZ. (*Picking up in intensity as he goes on.*) I have not finished! I was saying that place was entirely on my head and I had there the responsibility to keep order and keep those men from escaping and they kept trying and it was difficult to keep order there since the men kept trying. Naturally they had that right to try and I had my duty, which was to prevent them.

BAKER. But you did try to get relieved of that assignment, did you not?

WIRZ. Yes sir, I tried to do that. I wrote to General Winder, asking to be assigned to another post, but he informed me he could not relieve me. And, simply—I had there to stay and so it kept on being on my head.

BAKER. I have here a letter written by defendant to General Winder, dated May 19, 1864, in which defendant requests that he be relieved of his post at Andersonville.

SCHADE. (*Takes letter to Wallace.*) Submitted for the defense.

WALLACE. (*Glances at it.*) It may be entered.

SCHADE. (*Takes letter to Clerk.*) Letter of May 19th, 1864, offered for the defense.

CLERK. Exhibit ten for the defense.

BAKER. Capt. Wirz, did you strike down and kill a man called William Stewart?

WIRZ. (*Shouting.*) There was no William Stewart and that is a lie —— (*Wallace raps gavel . . . Wirz repeats sullenly.*) There was no William Stewart.

BAKER. Did you, at any time, shoot down or kill a prisoner of war?

WIRZ. No, sir; I never did that. I could not physically do that.

BAKER. Captain Wirz, when you were arrested at the conclusion of hostilities, were you making any attempt to escape?

WIRZ. No, sir; I saw no reason to do that. I was with my family outside the stockade and, having heard of the general pardon, was on my way back to Louisville when a Major—of General Wilson's forces entered to tell me I was under arrest. I was taken away and held prisoner. I soon understood the awful charge against me— and that my fate was to hang ——! (Baker abruptly tries to close off examination.)

BAKER. That will be all, thank you.

WIRZ. Am I not to be asked my conception of my duty?

BAKER. Thank you, Captain Wirz.

WIRZ. I wish to explain how I understand the military rules!

BAKER. Very well. Explain your understanding of the military code.

WIRZ. (With bite and growing bitterness.) That one does as he is ordered. That he keeps his feelings to himself. That he does not play the heroic game which some people who are not in his position think he could play. That he obeys. That he does not concern himself with the policies of his superiors,—but obeys. That he does his assigned job and obeys. That when the order to charge is given,—he obeys. That when ordered to keep prisoners,— he obeys. And if in so doing he must die, then he dies!

BAKER. Your witness, Colonel.

CHIPMAN. (Seated. After a long moment of silence.) You have explained your sense of your duty clearly, Mr. Wirz. When the officer is ordered to keep prisoners he obeys.

WIRZ. Yes, sir.

CHIPMAN. Meaning that he must keep the prisoners from escaping?

WIRZ. That is one of the things—yes.

CHIPMAN. Meaning that he must keep them alive ——?

WIRZ. As much as it is within his power.

CHIPMAN. Which did you regard as more important? To keep them from escaping or keep them alive?

WIRZ. According to the customs of war, to keep them alive as it was within my power and to prevent them from escaping.

CHIPMAN. One duty neither more nor less important in your mind?

WIRZ. Both equal ——

CHIPMAN. You say you never at any time killed a prisoner of war?

WIRZ. (Raising arms slightly.) It has been demonstrated that I could not ——

CHIPMAN. I ask you, sir, directly—did you or did you not ——?

WIRZ. I never did that. No, sir.

CHIPMAN. In that letter of May 26, 1864, in which you tell General Winder of your increasing duties at Andersonville I note that you also ask him to consider a promotion in rank for you from captain to major. What were you concerned with when you wrote that letter? The overcrowding or your promotion?

WIRZ. It was nothing wrong in the same letter to request that promotion ——

CHIPMAN. And in your letter requesting a transfer from Andersonville you make a point of your illness as the reason ——

WIRZ. To make it indirect otherwise General Wnider might not have liked that transfer request.

CHIPMAN. But you were in fact seeking medical attention when you wrote that letter, weren't you?

WIRZ. I had in mind at the same time to get away from that assignment.

CHIPMAN. You say that what occurred at Andersonville was beyond your power to avert?

WIRZ. Yes, sir.

CHIPMAN. In the course of performing your duties you inspected the stockade—at times I imagine from the wall where the sentries stood. You could look down into that—how would you describe it, may I ask?

WIRZ. It has been described ——

CHIPMAN. As a sort of hell ——?

WIRZ. Oh, indescribable, sir. Indescribable. I suppose you remember, Colonel, hearing me say that I could not bear the sight of those young boy prisoners in there, sixty to seventy of them, and sent them out to pick blackberries ——

CHIPMAN. That is in your favor ——

WIRZ. Thank you ——

CHIPMAN. It is interesting that you keep referring to that act— as if there is so much else you dare not remember ——
WIRZ. You twist things, sir—I let Father Whelan bring bread ——
CHIPMAN. You went to your duties from your home every morning?
WIRZ. Yes, sir.
CHIPMAN. And I take it you were a normal father and husband, concerned to raise your children properly and teaching them the common virtues ——?
WIRZ. Particularly in a religious way—yes.
CHIPMAN. And you saw nothing strange in leaving your family and your grace at meals to go to your job of overseeing the dying of those men?
BAKER. Objection!
CHIPMAN. Withdrawn. You have said that keeping those men alive was of equal importance in your mind with the need to keep them from escaping?
WIRZ. Yes, sir.
CHIPMAN. The food was wormy and rotten. Did you think of sending out foragers to commandeer supplies from Georgia farmers?
WIRZ. It would have been illegal ——
CHIPMAN. You could have signed vouchers ——
WIRZ. I was not authorized ——
CHIPMAN. Payable by the Confederacy ——
WIRZ. Not authorized, sir ——
CHIPMAN. Sent out squads of prisoners to collect firewood ——
WIRZ. They would escape ——
CHIPMAN. Under guard ——
WIRZ. There were not enough guards ——
CHIPMAN. Enlarged the stockade ——
WIRZ. The size was prescribed ——
CHIPMAN. Let those prisoners among whom were carpenters, masons, and mechanics of all sorts, build the shelters which would have kept them alive ——?
WIRZ. As I have already said—not authorized ——
CHIPMAN. But those measures would have saved lives ——
WIRZ. I don't know how many!! ——
CHIPMAN. (*Flaring.*) We will say only one! —— Would you say one, single human life is precious, Mr. Wirz?

WIRZ. I do not follow—it would have been illegal for me to do the things you say ——

CHIPMAN. But morally right, Mr. Wirz?

BAKER. Objection.

WALLACE. We do not see how the Judge Advocate's questioning connects with the charge of conspiracy.

CHIPMAN. (*Grimly.*) Will the Court allow me to explore that issue one step further before deciding the connection cannot be made?

WALLACE. (*With equal grimness.*) You may explore it—one step further.

CHIPMAN. Mr. Wirz, you are a religious man?

WIRZ. As I have testified—I know how important religion is, and I allowed all ministers ——

CHIPMAN. Then, sir, professing religion as you do, would you agree that moral considerations, the promptings of conscience, are primary for all men?

WIRZ. Of course I do! I observe that ideal like most men—when —I—can!

CHIPMAN. When you can. Then you could not observe moral considerations at Andersonville?

WIRZ. That situation was General Winder's responsibility—not mine.

CHIPMAN. (*Rising, moving closer to Wirz.*) You regarded that situation as General Winder's responsibility because he was your military superior?

WIRZ. Yes ——

CHIPMAN. And how far over did you deem his authority over you to extend?

WIRZ. To all circumstances, considering that was a military-war situation.

CHIPMAN. To all circumstances. Are you certain of that?

WIRZ. I am absolutely certain!

CHIPMAN. (*Advances slowly to Wirz.*) And had he, in that military-war situation, given you a direct order to slaughter one of your own children without giving you an explanation, would you have done that?

WIRZ. That is ridiculous ——

CHIPMAN. Would you have done that?

WIRZ. It's ridiculous—I do not answer ——

66

CHIPMAN. Would you have done that?

WIRZ. No ——!

CHIPMAN. Why not?

WIRZ. It would be an insane order ——!

CHIPMAN. Yes. Insane. Or inhuman. Or immoral. And a man therefore in his heart does indeed make some inner judgment as to the orders he obeys.

WALLACE. (*Gavel.*) The Judge Advocate will hold. The Court has stated more than once, it is not disposed to consider the moral issue relating to soldierly conduct. It has indicated to the Judge Advocate that we are on extremely delicate ground at any time that we enter into the circumstances under which officers may disobey their military superiors. However, the Judge Advocate apparently now feels he must enter that area. He will advance some legal basis for that line of questioning or withdraw it.

CHIPMAN. If it please the Court—we will endeavor to connect this line ——

WALLACE. The Judge Advocate must in advance furnish a legal basis ——

CHIPMAN. The Judge Advocate respectfully urges ——

WALLACE. (*Gavel.*) The Court must hear some basis for permitting this line of inquiry!

CHIPMAN. (*Crosses slowly to table,* L.) If it please the Court, military courts—judging war crimes—are governed by both the criminal code and by the broader, more general code of universal international law. In most cases that come before them, they will judge specific acts in which the nature and degree of offense is determinable without great difficulty. But, on rare occasions, cases occur demanding from a Court a more searching inquiry. Should the Court allow such broad inquiry it becomes more than the court of record in a particular case; it becomes a supreme tribunal —willing to peer into the very heart of human conduct. The Judge Advocate urges that the Court does not in advance limit or narrowly define the basis for questioning. Should the Court insist on such a basis, then we are through with the witness. (*Sits.*)

WALLACE. Does the Judge Advocate offer the Court alternatives?

CHIPMAN. We did not mean to imply that ——

WALLACE. The Court is flattered to think it may take on the mantle of a supreme tribunal—however, it is still a military court.

CHIPMAN. If it please the Court ——

67

WALLACE. No, Colonel, I'm not through. The Court grants that it may be philosophically true that men have the human right to judge the commands of their military superiors, but in practice one does so at his peril.

CHIPMAN. (*Slowly.*) At his peril, yes sir.

WALLACE. (*His tone is deadly.*) We would want that the peril of that line of questioning be understood most clearly. We have a question for the Judge Advocate that he may or may not answer—he is not, of course, on trial here. The question is: what is it an honest man fights for when he takes up arms for his country? Is it the state or the moral principle inherent in that state? And if the State and the principle are not one, is he bound not to fight for that state and indeed to fight against it? The Judge Advocate need not answer, for we will make the question more particular. If, at the outbreak of the war, the government of the so-called Confederacy had stood on the moral principle of freedom for the black man and the government of the United States had stood for slavery, would a man have been bound, on moral grounds, to follow the dictates of conscience—even if it had led him to the point of taking up arms against the government of the United States?

CHIPMAN. (*Anguished.*) It is inconceivable to me ——

WALLACE. That is not the question.

CHIPMAN. That situation could not possibly occur ——

WALLACE. That is not the question.

CHIPMAN. (*Bursting.*) He would have been bound to follow the dictates of his conscience.

WALLACE. Even to the point of taking up arms against the government of the United States?

CHIPMAN. (*After a pause, slow.*) Yes.

WALLACE. (*With deliberateness.*) The Colonel understands, of course, that a man must be prepared to pay the penalties involved in violating the—let us say—the code of the group to which he belongs. In other societies that has meant death. In our society it can mean merely deprivation of status—the contempt of his fellows—exile in the midst of his countrymen. I take it the Colonel understands my meaning?

CHIPMAN. He understands what the Court is saying.

WALLACE. And he still feels that he must enter that dangerous area?

CHIPMAN. (*Now he is pleading, no longer hard.*) General, I do not enter that area of my own free will. I enter because I have been forced to it by the nature of this case. (*Rises, crosses to above Generals.*) We have lately emerged from a terrible and bloody war and that war has spawned a most sinister and curious crime. Men in the thousands—fourteen thousand men—have been sent to their death—not by bullets on the battlefield, but in a subtle, furtive, hidden manner. We have in the course of this trial examined as it were the outward appearance of hell—its walls, deadline, swamp, dogs, its terrible heat and freezing cold. But we have not gotten to the heart of it. We are now faced with the necessity of exploring further into—let us say it again—hell. I put it to this Court that we owe to those fourteen thousand who died there—to those who mourn them—something so true as to put us head and shoulders above politics, above sectionalism, above the bitterness in our own hearts. I admit to entering this room with that bitterness in myself—I admit to the mood of vengeance. I would now wish to go beyond that if I can. As we say—life is precious —— As we cling to our humanity by our fingernails in this world—by our fingernails—let us have a human victory in this room.

WALLACE. (*After a pause.*) The Court is not unmoved. (*Long pause. The Judge leans toward Wallace whispering to him.*) The Judge Advocate considers as primary to the presentation of his case the moral issue of disobedience to a superior officer?

CHIPMAN. (*Strained. At table, L.*) Yes, sir.

WALLACE. (*Again the pause and then Wallace speaks almost angrily.*) The Judge Advocate may continue ——

BAKER. (*Rises.*) The Judge Advocate may continue? Defense counsel is amazed that the Court does not now recognize there is no legal case here. To attempt to connect normal obedience to orders with willful conspiracy is impossible and no fine sounding statement about universal law or supreme tribunal can bridge the unbridgeable. The Court knows the Judge Advocate cannot possibly make that connection. And yet the Court allows the Judge Advocate to proceed when it should forthwith dismiss the defendant ——

WALLACE. Is counsel ordering the Court to do that?

BAKER. No, but he submits there is no legal case here.

WALLACE. The Judge Advocate may continue— (*Baker sits.*) bearing in mind that the Court may conclude at any time it

69

feels there is nothing more to be gained from this line of questioning.

CHIPMAN. (*Crosses slowly to* R. *of Wirz.*) Mr. Wirz, we have said that a man does make some inner judgment as to the orders he obeys. That implies that if those orders offend his humanity deeply enough he may disobey them. The authority of General Winder over you was not absolute. And so the question is, why did you obey?

WIRZ. (*Sniffing disaster.*) Am I required to answer? . . . I did not think of my assignment at Andersonville in that way . . . (*Looking about him.*) I do not understand what happens here . . . I thought only in the normal way to obey him, since he was my military superior ——

CHIPMAN. (*To front of Generals—down, then to* R. *of Wirz.*) But not your *moral* superior. No man has authority over the soul of another. As we are men we own our own souls and as we own them we are equal as *men*—the general, the private, the professor, the hod-carrier. *We are equal as men, sir.* And every man alive as he is a man knows that—as you in your heart knew that ——

WIRZ. But that is not ——

CHIPMAN. And as that situation had become a grossly immoral situation, and as General Winder was not your moral superior, you did not have to obey him. So the question remains, *Why did you obey?* (*Wirz glances towards Wallace.*)

WALLACE. The Court will hear the answer.

WIRZ. (*Incredulously.*) I will say it clearly. I would have been most certainly court-martialed. And if my superiors wished, considering it was a time of war, and that the war had come to a desperate, bitter stage in which the word "traitor" could be sounded in a moment—I might have been executed ——

CHIPMAN. It might at least have been for a reason. You might have saved fourteen thousand lives—were you afraid?

WIRZ. I? A soldier? Afraid?

CHIPMAN. (*Above witness.*) The question then still is—*Why did you obey?*

WIRZ. As I have explained. What heroic thing do you demand I should have done at Andersonville? I—an ordinary man like most men?

CHIPMAN. (*Crosses slowly to table* L.) Mr. Wirz, we who are born into the human race are elected to an extraordinary role in the scheme of things. We are endowed with reason and therefore with personal responsibility for our acts. A man may give to officials over him many things. But not what is called his soul, sir—not his immortal soul. And the question therefore still is—*Why did you obey?*

WIRZ. Why? As I have said. As I say for the last time—it was to me a military situation.

CHIPMAN. (*Moves to front ⁀of Generals.*) But that was not a military situation, Mr. Wirz. Those helpless, unarmed men were no longer the enemy, whatever Winder said. Here was no longer a question of North and South; no longer a question of war; only a question of human beings. Chandler saw that. Those Southern women who brought food for those starving men—they saw that. Where was your conscience then? (*Crosses to table L.*)

WIRZ. Where!!??

CHIPMAN. In General Winder's pocket with his keys, his tobacco, and his money. And worth no more than any of those things ——

WIRZ. (*With controlled fury.*) You speak high, Colonel—high! Ask them in this room if they can say in their hearts they would have done different if they had been in my place—ask them. You are all the victors here and you make up a morality for the losers!

CHIPMAN. Yes! The victor makes the morality since the loser cannot.

WIRZ. And I spit on that morality! I spit on it! And I say—ask them in this room if they would have done different—ask them ——

CHIPMAN. (*Moves to Wirz.*) And if they could not, then we must shudder for the world we live in—to think what may happen when one man owns the conscience of many men. For the prospect before us is then a world of Andersonvilles—of jailers concerned only to execute the commands of their masters. (R. *of Wirz.*) And freed of his conscience—fearing only the authority to which he had surrendered his soul—*might the jailer not commit murder then?*

WIRZ. I did not commit murder!

CHIPMAN. (*Circles front of Wirz.*) You did not kill William Stewart?

WIRZ. There was no William Stewart ——

71

CHIPMAN. You were never in a fury with those men—a fury great enough to overcome the weakness of your arms?

WIRZ. It is as the doctors say ——

CHIPMAN. (*Crosses to* L. *of* Wirz.) To whom do you dare say that? You and I have been on the battlefield. We've seen men holding their bowels in their hands and with their legs broken, still moving forward. You raised your arms ——

WIRZ. No ——!

CHIPMAN. Yes! You were in a fury when you rode out to hunt down those men with that dogpack and when you caught them you raised those two dead arms ——

WIRZ. No ——!

CHIPMAN. (*Toward a cresendo.*) Then how did you rein that hardmouthed horse you rode to the left—and how to the right—and how bring his head down when he reared—if not with those two-dead-arms? (*He grabs* Wirz *by the upper arms and pulls him out of chair.* Wirz *cries out, and simultaneously,* Baker *and* Wallace *start, as if to speak, but* Chipman *lets go as quickly as he has taken hold, horrified by what he has done.*)

WIRZ. Possibly!—I raise my arms sometimes! Yes!—but I did not kill any William Stewart because there was no William Stewart, so help me God.

CHIPMAN. (*Crosses to front of couch—sits, stares at his hands. Both men are near exhaustion.*) We will leave Mr. Stewart aside—but you had to obey orders which you knew were killing men, didn't you?

WIRZ. I had to obey ——

CHIPMAN. Even though you knew that to obey was to kill those men—and to disobey was to save them?

WIRZ. (*Making a curiously helpless gesture.*) Even though —— Simply—I could not disobey. (*His anger is working up from a deep place.*) I did my duty as I saw it. I have made that clear. But you badger me. Which however way I explain it, it will not do for you—and you badger me—you badger me! I have made it clear that I had to keep order there. To keep the record monthly of the number of prisoners including those escaping—to report that to General Winder and the War Department—and you badger me. It has been made clear—and *you will not let go.* To prevent them from escaping—to report in writing the attempted escapes—that was my responsibility. Isn't that clear? Even though I had not enough men, that did not excuse me, though I found that job overwhelming—isn't that clear? And you badger me! It *was* overwhelming and I had to find ways and means to block those escape attempts—that was my duty. It was solely on my head. So it went, I preventing, they trying, I preventing, they trying. And no move to stop them completely successful. Nothing, nothing could stop them. And that responsibility solely mine. The dead-line—that did not prevent them. Cannon mounted on the wall— that did not prevent them. They kept trying. Tunnelling under the walls. Digging, burrowing, burrowing —— In the night, burrowing. Crushed from the weight of the wall timbers when they made the mistake to burrow directly under those logs. And the others continuing. Continuing. Tracked down by the dogs and trying again . . . and I having to anticipate . . . finding their tunnels . . . learning their tricks. They trying, I preventing. They trying, I preventing. They bribing the guards with greenbacks . . . blacking their faces to pass as niggers to bring the dead bodies out of the stockade . . . and I charged to block those moves. But nothing prevents them to try . . . that burrowing. At night. I'm awake. I don't need to see them to know what they are doing. Burrowing. In the night. Digging, digging, in that hopeless effort to escape, digging, crawling—like rats ——

CHIPMAN. And rats may die and one may have no compunction about rats ——

WIRZ. Yes—I meant rats, so to speak —— You are playing a cheap lawyer's trick on me ——

CHIPMAN. Very well, a cheap lawyer's trick—so they were not rats to you—*but they were no longer men to you.* In your mind you cancelled them out as men and you made them less than men, and then they might die and one did not have to suffer over that, did he? (*Almost gently.*) Why did you try to commit suicide in your cell? (*Wirz is silent.*) Is it because you feel nothing? (*Silence*). Is it because you have no human feeling left and cannot endure yourself feeling nothing? (*Silence.*) You speak too much of your children . . . ! Is it because you have already—in your mind—asked them—"Should I have done my duty, or should I have given a man a drink of water?"—And you heard their answer. (*Wirz starts.*) Yes —— You wish to die. (*Rises, crosses to* R. *of Wirz. His tone is one of pained exhausted inquiry—no longer hunting.*) I ask you for the last time, Mr. Wirz, Why—and it was not fear of court-martial or dismissal or any external thing—why—*inside* yourself—couldn't you disobey?

WIRZ. (*In a low relieved exhalation.*) Simply—I—could not. I did not have that feeling in myself to be able to. I did not have that feeling of strength to do that. I—could—not—disobey.

CHIPMAN. (*With dragging feet, exhausted, crosses to table.*) The government rests. (*Fast dim to out. Wirz moves to standing position below foot of couch to await sentencing. When ready, Wallace's voice is heard in the dark and the lights slowly come back up.*)

ACT II

SCENE 2

The following day.

WALLACE. (*Finishing.*) . . . and on the charge that the prisoner did with others conspire to destroy the lives of soldiers in the military service of the United States in violation of the laws and customs of war—Guilty. And on the various specifications that he aided and abetted murder and did commit murder—Guilty. And the Court do therefore sentence him, the said Henry Wirz, to be hanged by the neck till he be dead, at such time and place as the President of the United States may direct, two-thirds of the members of the Court concurring therein. The business of this military court being now terminated, we declare the Court dissolved. (*The gavel raps once. Wirz is led out. The Judges go out quickly. The general exit follows. Baker, with Schade at his shoulder, crosses to Chipman.*)

BAKER. I'll say this for you, Colonel. At least you fought on your own terms.

CHIPMAN. I asked for Wirz' guilt—not his death.

BAKER. But he dies anyway. His life for the Union dead. No matter that you so stubbornly fought to purify the occasion—it was a political verdict whatever you said.

CHIPMAN. I charged him for what he is. Perhaps, deep down, the Court did, too.

BAKER. Perhaps. It was a worthy effort though it hasn't anything to do with the real world. Men will go on as they are, most of them, subject to fear—and so subject to powers and authorities. And how are we to change *that* slavery? When it's of man's very nature?

CHIPMAN. Is it?

BAKER. Isn't it?

CHIPMAN. I don't know. We try.

BAKER. (*Ironically.*) We redecorate the beast in all sorts of political coats, hoping that we change him, but is he to be changed?

CHIPMAN. We try. We try. (*Baker goes out, followed by Hosmer and Schade. A moment later, Chipman leaves, walking slowly. The lights dim, leaving only a light on the Andersonville map which fades slowly as the*

CURTAIN FALLS

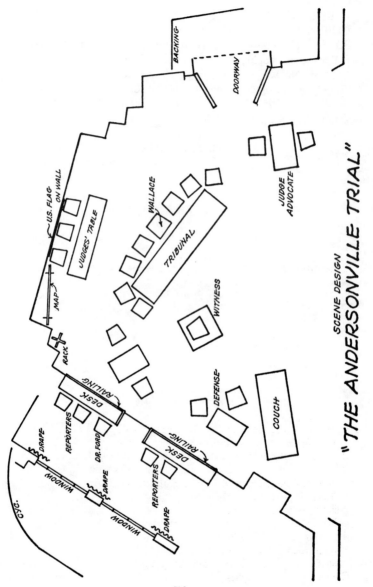

SCENE DESIGN
"THE ANDERSONVILLE TRIAL"

PROPERTY PLOT

Curtains—2 pairs
25 chairs
Small table
Stool
Victorian chaise
Gavel
Doctor's bag
Pistol
2 watch fobs
2 watches and chains
6 pillows
Chandelier

5 shades
3 large sconces
Ink wells, pads, etc.
Quill feathers
Books
Blue covers
Ink markers
Civil War papers and letters
Bible
Board pointer
Large table
2 rifles

COSTUME PLOT

Baker: Beige 2-piece suit, grey and black stripe vest
Baker: Tan and white stripe 3-piece suit
Chipman and Union soldiers: 2 navy vests
Wirz: Black 3-piece suit
Bates: Grey coat, grey mixed pants, orange vest
Chandler: Tan coat and pants, brown vest
Spencer: Rust coat, orange pants, grey vest, padding
Sgt. Gray: Sergeant's coat, gold stripes
Schade:
Black 2-piece suit
  Act I: black vest
  Act II: grey vest
Court Clerk and Stenographer: 2 sergeant's jackets, white stripes
Union soldiers: 2 soldier jackets
Reporter: Rust coat and pants, brown vest
Reporter: Grey mix coat, brown check pants, grey vest
Culver: Corduroy jacket, light blue pants (torn)
Officers: 15 long navy coats
Officers: 6 pairs navy pants
Officers and Soldiers: 12 pairs light blue pants
All civilians: 7 civilian hats
Ford, Williams, Lieutenant: 3 Cavalry hats
Soldiers, Gray, Culver, and Davidson: 5 caps
Generals: 4 yellow sashes

Officers: 2 red sashes
Civilians: 14 dickies
Chipman and Civilians: 18 ties (Black bow—Chipman and
Union soldiers), 29 pairs shoes (28 black, 1 brown)
29 pairs shoes (28 black, 1 brown)
Sgt. Gray: 1 pair boots
17 belts
Extra-Baker: Grey tweed 3-piece suit
Wirz and Union soldiers: Dark grey mixed 3-piece suit
Extra: Rust colored pants and vest
Extra: Beige vest
Baker and Union soldiers: Light grey linen suit 3-piece
Reporter: Brown jacket, tan pants, tan vest
Reporter: Grey mix coat, grey vest, black pants
Reporter: Brown stripe 3-piece suit
Reporter: Brown check coat and pants, tan vest
Chipman: 5 white shirts—15-5
Chipman: 5 white shirts—16-4
Baker: 5 beige shirts—16½-7
Culver: 2 blue shirts—15-2
Davidson: 2 brown print shirts—14½-3
Wirz and Union soldiers: 1 beige shirt—16-2
Culver: Navy jacket, grey vest, red check pants

INDIVIDUAL COSTUME PLOT

General Wallace—long coat, navy pants, yellow sash, belt

Lieutenant—long coat, light blue pants, belt, cavalry hat

Court Clerk—Sergeant's coat (white stripes), light blue pants

Court Reporter—Sergeant's coat (white stripes), light blue pants

Chipman—long coat, light blue pants, belt, heavy vest, white shirt (round collar), black bow tie

Baker—

    Act I: beige suit, grey and black vest, beige shirt, green or dark blue string tie

    Act II: tan and white stripe 3-piece suit, beige shirt, green or dark blue string tie

Capt. Williams—long coat, light blue pants, cavalry hat, belt

Wirz—black 3-piece suit, white shirt, black string tie

Schade—black 2-piece suit, dickie, tie. Act I: black vest, Act II: grey vest, black hat

Chandler—tan coat and pants, brown vest, dickie, black tie, brown hat

Bates—grey coat, orange vest, grey tweed pants, dickie, brown tie, black bowler hat

Spencer—rust coat, grey vest, orange pants, dickie, brown tie, brown derby

Ford—long coat, light blue pants with green stripe, belt, cavalry hat

Hosmer—long coat, light blue pants, belt

Davidson—corduroy jacket, light blue pants (torn), brown print shirt, belt, cap

Culver—dark blue jacket, grey vest, red check pants, light blue shirt, cap

Sgt. Gray—short jacket, (gold stripes) light blue pants (yellow stripe), boots, cap

Union soldiers—short jackets, light blue pants (no stripe), caps, belts

Reporters—civilian clothes

General Mott—long coat, dark pants, belt, yellow sash

General Thomas—long coat, dark pants, belt, yellow sash

General Geary—long coat, dark pants, belt, yellow sash

General Fessenden—long coat, dark pants, belt, yellow sash

General Ballier—long coat, dark pants, belt, yellow sash

Colonel Allcock—long coat, light blue pants, red sash, belt

NEW PLAYS

★ **INTIMATE APPAREL by Lynn Nottage.** The moving and lyrical story of a turn-of-the-century black seamstress whose gifted hands and sewing machine are the tools she uses to fashion her dreams from the whole cloth of her life's experiences. "…Nottage's play has a delicacy and eloquence that seem absolutely right for the time she is depicting…" –*NY Daily News.* "…thoughtful, affecting…The play offers poignant commentary on an era when the cut and color of one's dress—and of course, skin—determined whom one could and could not marry, sleep with, even talk to in public." –*Variety.* [2M, 4W] ISBN: 0-8222-2009-1

★ **BROOKLYN BOY by Donald Margulies.** A witty and insightful look at what happens to a writer when his novel hits the bestseller list. "The characters are beautifully drawn, the dialogue sparkles…" –*nytheatre.com.* "Few playwrights have the mastery to smartly investigate so much through a laugh-out-loud comedy that combines the vintage subject matter of successful writer-returning-to-ethnic-roots with the familiar mid-life crisis." –*Show Business Weekly.* [4M, 3W] ISBN: 0-8222-2074-1

★ **CROWNS by Regina Taylor.** Hats become a springboard for an exploration of black history and identity in this celebratory musical play. "Taylor pulls off a Hat Trick: She scores thrice, turning CROWNS into an artful amalgamation of oral history, fashion show, and musical theater…" –*TheatreMania.com.* "…wholly theatrical…Ms. Taylor has created a show that seems to arise out of spontaneous combustion, as if a bevy of department-store customers simultaneously decided to stage a revival meeting in the changing room." –*NY Times.* [1M, 6W (2 musicians)] ISBN: 0-8222-1963-8

★ **EXITS AND ENTRANCES by Athol Fugard.** The story of a relationship between a young playwright on the threshold of his career and an aging actor who has reached the end of his. "[Fugard] can say more with a single line than most playwrights convey in an entire script…Paraphrasing the title, it's safe to say this drama, making its memorable entrance into our consciousness, is unlikely to exit as long as a theater exists for exceptional work." –*Variety.* "A thought-provoking, elegant and engrossing new play…" –*Hollywood Reporter.* [2M] ISBN: 0-8222-2041-5

★ **BUG by Tracy Letts.** A thriller featuring a pair of star-crossed lovers in an Oklahoma City motel facing a bug invasion, paranoia, conspiracy theories and twisted psychological motives. "…obscenely exciting…top-flight craftsmanship. Buckle up and brace yourself…" –*NY Times.* "…[a] thoroughly outrageous and thoroughly entertaining play…the possibility of enemies, real and imagined, to squash has never been more theatrical." –*A.P.* [3M, 2W] ISBN: 0-8222-2016-4

★ **THOM PAIN (BASED ON NOTHING) by Will Eno.** An ordinary man muses on childhood, yearning, disappointment and loss, as he draws the audience into his last-ditch plea for empathy and enlightenment. "It's one of those treasured nights in the theater—treasured nights anywhere, for that matter—that can leave you both breathless with exhilaration and…in a puddle of tears." –*NY Times.* "Eno's words…are familiar, but proffered in a way that is constantly contradictory to our expectations. Beckett is certainly among his literary ancestors." –*nytheatre.com.* [1M] ISBN: 0-8222-2076-8

★ **THE LONG CHRISTMAS RIDE HOME by Paula Vogel.** Past, present and future collide on a snowy Christmas Eve for a troubled family of five. "…[a] lovely and hauntingly original family drama…a work that breathes so much life into the theater." –*Time Out.* "…[a] delicate visual feast…" –*NY Times.* "…brutal and lovely…the overall effect is magical." –*NY Newsday.* [3M, 3W] ISBN: 0-8222-2003-2

DRAMATISTS PLAY SERVICE, INC.
440 Park Avenue South, New York, NY 10016 212-683-8960 Fax 212-213-1539
postmaster@dramatists.com   www.dramatists.com